The Tyndale New Testament Commentaries

General Editor:
THE REV. CANON LEON MORRIS, M.Sc., M.Th., Ph.D.

1 AND 2 THESSALONIANS

THE EPISTLES OF PAUL TO THE THESSALONIANS

AN INTRODUCTION AND COMMENTARY

by

THE REV. CANON LEON MORRIS
M.Sc., M.Th., Ph.D.

Inter-Varsity Press,
Leicester, England

William B. Eerdmans Publishing Company
Grand Rapids, Michigan

Inter-Varsity Press
38 De Montfort Street, Leicester LE1 7GP, England
Wm. B. Eerdmans Publishing Company
255 Jefferson S.E., Grand Rapids, MI 49503

Published and sold only in the USA and Canada by Wm. B. Eerdmans Publishing Co.

Unless otherwise stated, quotations from the Bible are taken from the New International Version, © 1978 by New York International Bible Society, published in Great Britain by Hodder and Stoughton Ltd.

British Library Cataloguing in Publication Data

Morris, Leon
The Epistles of Paul to the Thessalonians.
—2nd ed. — (Tyndale New Testament
commentaries; v. 13)
1. Bible. N.T. — Thessalonians — Commentaries
I. Title   II. Series
227'.807   BS 2725.3

ISBN 0-85111-882-8

Reprinted, December 1991

Library of Congress Cataloging in Publication Data

Morris, Leon, 1914-
The Epistles of Paul to the Thessalonians.

(The Tyndale New Testament commentaries)
1. Bible.   N.T. Thessalonians — Commentaries.
I. Title.   II. Series.
BS2725.3.M67   1984   227'.8106   84-12839

ISBN 0-8028-0034-3 (Eerdmans)

Set in Palatino. Typeset in Great Britain by Input Typesetting Ltd., London.
Printed in U.S.A. by Eerdmans Printing Company, Grand Rapids, Michigan.

Inter-Varsity Press is the publishing division of the Universities and Colleges Christian Fellowship (formerly the Inter-Varsity Fellowship), a student movement linking Christian Unions in universities and colleges throughout the United Kingdom and the Republic of Ireland, and a member movement of the International Fellowship of Evangelical Students. For information about local and national activities write to UCCF, 38 De Montfort Street, Leicester LE1 7GP.

GENERAL PREFACE

The original *Tyndale Commentaries* aimed at providing help for the general reader of the Bible. They concentrated on the meaning of the text without going into scholarly technicalities. They sought to avoid 'the extremes of being unduly technical or unhelpfully brief'. Most who have used the books agree that there has been a fair measure of success in reaching that aim.

Times, however, change. A series that has served so well for so long is perhaps not quite as relevant as when it was first launched. New knowledge has come to light. The discussion of critical questions has moved on. Bible-reading habits have changed. When the original series was commenced it could be presumed that most readers used the Authorized Version and one could make one's comments accordingly, but this situation no longer obtains.

The decision to revise and up-date the whole series was not reached lightly, but in the end it was thought that this is what is required in the present situation. There are new needs, and they will be better served by new books or by a thorough up-dating of the old books. The aims of the original series remain. The new commentaries are neither minuscule nor unduly long. They are exegetical rather than homiletic. They do not discuss all the critical questions, but none is written without an awareness of the problems that engage the attention of New Testament scholars. Where it is felt that formal consideration should be given to such questions, they are discussed in the Introduction and sometimes in Additional Notes.

But the main thrust of these commentaries is not critical. These books are written to help the non-technical reader to understand his Bible better. They do not presume a knowledge of Greek, and all Greek words discussed are transliterated; but the authors have the Greek text before them and their comments are made on the basis of the originals. The authors are free to choose their own modern translation, but are asked to bear in mind the variety of translations in current use.

The new series of *Tyndale Commentaries* goes forth, as the former series did, in the hope that God will graciously use these books to help the general reader to understand as fully and clearly as possible the meaning of the New Testament.

LEON MORRIS

CONTENTS

7

AUTHOR'S PREFACE TO THE FIRST EDITION

The Epistles to the Thessalonians are all too little studied today. It may be true that they lack the theological profundity of Romans and the exciting controversy of Galatians; but nevertheless their place in Scripture is an important one. No other writing of the great apostle provides a greater insight into his missionary methods and message. Here we see Paul the missionary and Paul the pastor, faithfully proclaiming the gospel of God, concerned for the welfare of his converts, scolding them, praising them, guiding them, exhorting them, teaching them; thrilled with their progress, disappointed with their slowness. Though the continuous exposition of great doctrines is not a characteristic of the Thessalonian writings, yet it is fascinating to see how most, if not all, of the great Pauline doctrines are present, either by implication or direct mention. When we consider the undoubtedly early date of these letters this is a fact of importance in the history of Christian thought.

Especially important is the teaching of these Epistles on eschatology; and in view of the revival of interest in this doctrine in recent times it is imperative that we understand and appreciate the contribution of Thessalonians to this difficult subject. It is my earnest hope that this short commentary may help to direct the attention of Christian people to the importance of these Epistles and the relevance of their message for the men of today.

Every commentator, I suppose, bases his work on that of his predecessors, and in this I am certainly no exception. I have learned much from those who have written on these Epistles before me, and cannot hope to have acknowledged all my indebtednesses. I have found particularly helpful the commentaries by Milligan, Frame (*I.C.C.*), Denney (*Expositor's Bible*), Findlay (who wrote two commentaries, one in the *Cambridge Bible for Schools and Colleges*, and the other in the *Cambridge Greek Testament* series), and Neil (*Moffatt New Testament Commentary*), while Lightfoot's *Notes on Epistles of St Paul* is a veritable treasure-house.

Finally may I express my indebtedness to a number of my friends who have interested themselves in this project and made helpful suggestions. Especially am I indebted to the Very Rev. Dr S. Barton Babbage, the Rev. David Livingstone, and Mr I. Siggins, who read the typescript, and suggested many improvements.

LEON MORRIS

PREFACE TO THE SECOND EDITION

In the years since this commentary first appeared there have been some notable contributions to the literature on these Epistles, particularly the great commentaries by Rigaux in French and Best in English. I am grateful to both, and also to those who produced smaller commentaries, such as Ward, Moore, Whiteley and Bruce. These and others have been a great help to me as I worked over the material again. I have indicated my principal indebtednesses in the footnotes.

The revision has also enabled me to re-write the whole and there are many minor verbal alterations. Some things have been omitted as being of less importance now than in 1956 and this has given me space to include new material. Substantially this is the commentary I wrote in the 1950s, but I trust improved by what I have learned from the scholars I have mentioned and others. The English version used is the New International Version. I trust that in this new form this little book will prove useful to another generation of readers.

I am grateful to Mrs Dorothy Wellington, my former secretary, for her expert typing of the manuscript.

LEON MORRIS

CHIEF ABBREVIATIONS

Amp.	The Amplified Bible, 1965.
AV	The Authorized (or King James') Version.
BAGD	William F. Arndt and F. Wilbur Gingrich (eds.), *A Greek–English Lexicon of the New Testament and Other Early Christian Literature* (trans. of W. Bauer, *Griechisch-Deutsches Wörterbuch*), second edn. rev. and augmented by F. Wilbur Gingrich and Frederick W. Danker (University of Chicago Press, 1979).
Bailey	John W. Bailey, *The First and Second Epistles to the Thessalonians* (Abingdon, 1955); *The Interpreter's Bible*, vol. 11).
Barclay	William Barclay, *The Letters to the Philippians, Colossians and Thessalonians* (Saint Andrew Press, ²1960; *Daily Study Bible*).
BDF	F. Blass and A. Debrunner, *A Greek Grammar of the New Testament*, trans. and rev. by R. W. Funk (Cambridge, 1961).
Best	Ernest Best, *A Commentary on the First and Second Epistles to the Thessalonians* (Black, 1977; *Black's New Testament Commentaries*).
Bicknell	E. J. Bicknell, *The First and Second Epistles to the Thessalonians* (Methuen, 1932; *Westminster Commentary*).
BJRL	*Bulletin of the John Rylands Library*.
Bruce	F. F. Bruce, *1 & 2 Thessalonians* (Word, 1982; *Word Biblical Commentary*).
Calvin	John Calvin, *Commentaries on the Epistles of Paul*

the Apostle to the Philippians, Colossians, and Thessalonians, trans. John Pringle (Eerdmans reprint, 1948).

CBSC   G. G. Findlay, *The Epistles to the Thessalonians* (Cambridge, 1891; *The Cambridge Bible for Schools and Colleges*).

CGT   G. G. Findlay, *The Epistles of Paul the Apostle to the Thessalonians* (Cambridge, 1904; *The Cambridge Greek Testament*).

Denney   James Denney, *The Epistles to the Thessalonians* (Hodder and Stoughton, n.d.; *The Expositor's Bible*).

EB   *Encyclopaedia Biblica* (Black, 1914).

EGT   W. Robertson Nicoll (ed.), *The Expositor's Greek Testament,* vol. 4 (Eerdmans reprint, 1979).

EQ   *The Evangelical Quarterly.*

Frame   James Everett Frame, *A Critical and Exegetical Commentary on the Epistles of St. Paul to the Thessalonians* (T. & T. Clark, 1912; *International Critical Commentary*).

GNB   Good News Bible (Today's English Version), 1976.

GT   *A Greek–English Lexicon of the New Testament,* being Grimm's Wilke's *Clavis Novi Testamenti,* trans. and rev. by J. H. Thayer (T. & T. Clark, 1888).

HDB   James Hastings (ed.), *A Dictionary of the Bible,* 5 vols. (T. & T. Clark, 1898–1904).

Hendriksen   William Hendriksen, *New Testament Commentary Exposition of I and II Thessalonians* (Baker, 1955).

IB   *The Interpreter's Bible,* vol. 11 (Abingdon, 1955).

IBNTG   C. F. D. Moule, *Idiom Book of New Testament Greek* (Cambridge University Press, 1959).

IDB   *The Interpreter's Dictionary of the Bible,* 4 vols. (Abingdon, 1962); supplementary volume (1976).

ISBE   *The International Standard Bible Encyclopaedia,* 5 vols. (Howard Severance, 1929; rev. edn., 4 vols., Eerdmans, 1979–).

JB   The Jerusalem Bible, 1966.

Jowett	Benjamin Jowett, *The Epistles of St. Paul to the Thessalonians, Galatians and Romans*, vol. 1 (Murray, 1894).
LAE	Adolf Deissmann, *Light from the Ancient East* (Hodder and Stoughton, 1927).
LB	The Living Bible, 1971.
Lightfoot	J. B. Lightfoot, *Notes on Epistles of St Paul* (Macmillan, ²1904).
LSJ	H. G. Liddell and R. Scott, *A Greek–English Lexicon*, new ed. H. S. Jones and R. McKenzie, 2 vols. (Oxford, 1940).
LXX	The Septuagint.
Masson	Charles Masson, *Les Deux Épîtres de Saint Paul aux Thessaloniciens* (Delachaux et Niestlé, 1957).
mg.	margin
Milligan	George Milligan, *St Paul's Epistles to the Thessalonians* (Macmillan, 1908).
MM	James Hope Moulton and George Milligan, *The Vocabulary of the Greek Testament* (Hodder and Stoughton, 1914–29).
Moffatt	James Moffatt, *The New Testament. A New Translation* (Hodder and Stoughton, 1935).
Moore	A. L. Moore, *1 and 2 Thessalonians* (Nelson, 1969).
MS(S)	Manuscript(s).
NASB	The New American Standard Bible, 1963.
NBC	*New Bible Commentary*, ed. D. Guthrie *et al.* (Inter-Varsity Press, ³1970).
NBD	*New Bible Dictionary*, ed. J. D. Douglas *et al.* (Inter-Varsity Press, ²1982).
NEB	The New English Bible, Old Testament 1970; New Testament, ²1970.
Neil	William Neil, *The Epistles of Paul to the Thessalonians* (Hodder and Stoughton, 1950; *Moffatt New Testament Commentaries*).
NIV	The Holy Bible, New International Version, 1978.
NTS	*New Testament Studies.*
Phillips	J. B. Phillips, *Letters to Young Churches* (Bles, 1947).
Plummer I	Alfred Plummer, *A Commentary on St. Paul's First Epistle to the Thessalonians* (Scott, 1918).

Plummer II	Alfred Plummer, *A Commentary on St. Paul's Second Epistle to the Thessalonians* (Scott, 1918).
Poole	Matthew Poole, *A Commentary on the Holy Bible*, vol. 3 (Banner of Truth, 1963; reprint of 1685 edn.).
Rigaux	B. Rigaux, *Les Épîtres aux Thessaloniciens* (Gabalda, 1956; *Études Bibliques*).
Rolston	H. Rolston, *Thessalonians Timothy Titus Philemon* (SCM, 1963).
RSV	The Holy Bible, Revised Standard Version, Old Testament, 1952; New Testament, ²1971.
Rutherford	W. G. Rutherford, *St. Paul's Epistles to the Thessalonians and to the Corinthians, A New Translation* (Macmillan, 1908).
Samuel	Leith Samuel, *Awaiting Christ's Return* (Marshall, Morgan & Scott, 1961).
Schlier	Heinrich Schlier, *Der Apostel und seine Gemeinde* (Herder, 1972).
Simeon	Charles Simeon, *Horae Homileticae*, vol. 18 (Bohn, 1847).
TDNT	*Theological Dictionary of the New Testament*, trans. by Geoffrey W. Bromiley of *Theologisches Wörterbuch zum neuen Testament*, 10 vols. (Eerdmans, 1964–76).
Thomas	Robert L. Thomas, in *The Expositor's Bible Commentary*, ed. Frank E. Gaebelein, vol. 11 (Zondervan, 1978).
Ward	Ronald A. Ward, *Commentary on 1 & 2 Thessalonians* (Word, 1973).
Way	Arthur S. Way, *The Letters of St. Paul* (Macmillan, ⁵1921).
Whiteley	D. E. H. Whiteley, *Thessalonians in the Revised Standard Version* (Oxford, 1969).
Wilson	Geoffrey B. Wilson, *1 & 2 Thessalonians* (Banner of Truth, 1975).

INTRODUCTION

I. BACKGROUND

Thessalonica in the first century was the capital of Macedonia and its largest city. The geographical importance of its site may be gauged from the fact that Thessaloniki (until 1937, Salonika[1]) is still an important city. It is usually said that the name of the city in earlier days was Therma (from its hot springs), and that c. 315 BC it was renamed by Cassander after his wife Thessalonica, half-sister to Alexander the Great. But as the elder Pliny refers to Therma and Thessalonica as existing together,[2] it would seem that Cassander founded a new town which in due course extended and swallowed up the more ancient one nearby. Under the Romans it was the capital of the second of the four divisions of Macedonia, and when these were united to form one single province in 146 BC it became the capital, as well as the largest city of the province. Thessalonica was a free city, and inscriptions confirm the accuracy of Luke in calling its rulers 'politarchs'. It was strategically situated on the Via Egnatia, the great Roman highway to the East.

To this city came Paul in company with Silas and Timothy. The former was Paul's partner on his second missionary journey, chosen after the great apostle had separated from Barnabas. We first read of him when he and Judas Barsabbas, 'leaders among the brothers' and 'prophets' (Acts 15:22, 32), were sent to Antioch after the council of Jerusalem to convey to the believers there, both by letter and by word of mouth, the decisions the council had taken. He accompanied Paul on that apostle's

---

[1] See *The Statesman's Year Book 1938*, p. 1002, n. 1.
[2] Pliny, *Natural History* iv. 17.

second missionary journey, and Paul makes approving mention of his preaching (2 Cor.1:19). In later times he was associated with Peter in the writing of 1 Peter (1 Pet. 5:12). It is interesting that Paul and Peter both use the more formal name Silvanus, while Luke calls him Silas (perhaps Latin and Greek forms of a Semitic name, BDF, 125 (2)).

Timothy first comes under notice when Paul met him at Lystra and had him circumcised as a preliminary to his accompanying the apostle for the remainder of his second missionary journey (Acts 16:1–3). He came to be closely associated with Paul, as we see from the joint salutations in 2 Corinthians, Philippians, Colossians, 1 and 2 Thessalonians and Philemon. From the general tone of references to him we gather that Timothy was somewhat timid in disposition (cf. 1 Cor. 16:10). But he was high in Paul's confidence, for Paul sent him on missions (Acts 19:22; 1 Cor. 4:17; Phil. 2:19), and could link his preaching with his own (2 Cor. 1:19). Paul speaks warmly of Timothy's attitude to those to whom he ministered and to Paul himself (Phil. 2:20–22).

The three men preached at Philippi, but were compelled to leave after the imprisonment of Paul and Silas (Acts 16). They then came to Thessalonica, where Paul followed his usual practice of going to the synagogue. He preached there on three (apparently successive) sabbaths (Acts 17:2), with some success. His converts included some Jews, 'a large number' of devout Greeks, and 'not a few' chief women (Acts 17:4).[1] The chief success of the mission clearly lay among those Greeks who had attached themselves to the synagogue. These people were dissatisfied with the low standards of pagan morality and with the idol worship that fostered them. They were attracted by the monotheism and lofty morality of Judaism, but repelled by its narrow nationalism and ritual requirements. In Christianity they found a faith that satisfied. Some of the converts came of high-class families, but it is probable that most were from the lower classes, for Paul stresses his refusal to be dependent on

[1] This harmonizes with the fact that in Macedonia women had rather more liberty than elsewhere. See J. B. Lightfoot, *Saint Paul's Epistle to the Philippians* (Macmillan, ⁴1885), pp. 55–57; W. M. Ramsay, *St. Paul the Traveller and Roman Citizen* (Hodder and Stoughton, ¹⁴1930), p. 227.

them in any way (1 Thes. 2:9), and his letters to them contain no warnings about the dangers of riches.

The Jewish community did not take kindly to losing a considerable number of adherents. They reacted with violence and incited the rabble to attack the house of Jason, Paul's host (Acts 17:5). The mob took Jason before the politarchs, complaining that he had lodged those who 'have caused trouble all over the world' (Acts 17:6), and that the preachers had acted contrary to Caesar's laws in declaring Jesus to be another king (Acts 17:7). This is the first record of such an accusation since Jesus was brought before Pilate. It may be an echo of Paul's preaching of the second coming, which would agree with what we read in the Epistles. The politarchs took security of Jason and some others unnamed, and let them go.

It is not clear to what Jason and the others were bound. T. W. Manson and others think it was 'not to harbour seditious persons';[1] but this goes beyond what Acts says. K. and S. Lake think of Paul as having in effect 'jumped his bail'[2] when he left the city, but this is pure assumption. Frame is of the opinion that the security had nothing to do with Paul's absence, since the converts were surprised at his failure to return.[3] But the evidence for this surprise does not seem at all adequate, though it should be said that Paul envisaged a return (1 Thes. 2:17–18), which makes it unlikely that Jason undertook that he would stay away. Our best conjecture is that Jason and the other Christians were bound over to keep the peace, and that, in the troubled state of the moment, all were agreed that it would be better for Paul and Silas to leave immediately, at least for a time.

From Thessalonica they proceeded to Berea, where their preaching was successful until Thessalonian Jews followed them and stirred up such opposition that Paul was compelled to leave (Acts 17:13–14). He went to Corinth, where Silas and Timothy joined him (Acts 18:5). Timothy had previously come to Paul in Athens and then been sent back to Thessalonica (1 Thes. 3:2). It was on his return from this second visit to the

---

[1] *BJRL* 35, 1952–53, p. 432.
[2] K. and S. Lake, *An Introduction to the New Testament* (Christophers, ²1938), p. 135.
[3] Frame, p. 4.

city that he joined Paul at Corinth.

Up to this point Paul had had little to encourage him. In four successive centres there had been discouragement: a promising beginning had been followed by forcible disruption in Philippi, Thessalonica and Berea, and he had had little success in Athens. Small wonder that he began his preaching at Corinth 'in weakness and fear, and with much trembling' (1 Cor. 2:3). But when the messengers came from Thessalonica they brought such a report of the continuing steadfastness of the converts that Paul saw that the blessing of God had after all rested on his work there. His spirits rose and he gave himself much more energetically to his preaching. This appears to be the meaning of 'Paul devoted himself exclusively to preaching, testifying to the Jews that Jesus was the Christ' (Acts 18:5). Out of this sense of relief and reassurance the apostle wrote his first letter to the Thessalonians.

There are some later contacts with this church. Paul sent Timothy and Erastus to Macedonia (Acts 19:22), and he himself made two visits to the region (Acts 20:1–3). Some of the Thessalonians became his travelling companions, for example Aristarchus (Acts 19:29; 20:4; 27:2), Secundus (Acts 20:4), and perhaps Demas (2 Tim. 4:10; Phm. 24).

II. DATE OF COMPOSITION OF 1 THESSALONIANS

This letter was clearly written not long after Timothy came to Paul (1 Thes. 3:6; *cf.* 2:17). This meeting may have been the one that took place in Athens (1 Thes. 3:1–2), but is more probably that in Corinth (Acts 18:5), for the longer period seems necessary for the situation in Thessalonica to develop to the point where advice of the kind Paul gives was necessary. The longer period seems also to agree better with the fact that, by the time the letter was written, the faith of the Thessalonians was 'known everywhere' (1 Thes. 1:8).[1]

While Paul was in Corinth he was arrested and brought before

[1] W. G. Kümmel thinks that 'several months, but not more' seem to lie between Paul's departure from the city and the writing of this letter (*Introduction to the New Testament* (SCM, 1966), p. 184).

Gallio, the proconsul of Achaia (Acts 18:12). Now an inscription at Delphi, dealing with a question referred to the Emperor Claudius by this same Gallio, is dated in the twelfth year of the Emperor's tribunicial power and after his twenty-sixth acclamation as Emperor. This twelfth year was from 25th January 52 to 24th January 53; and, while the date of the twenty-sixth acclamation is not known exactly, the twenty-seventh was before 1st August 52. Thus Claudius' decision would have been given to Gallio during the first half of 52. Proconsuls usually took office in early summer and held office for one year. It thus seems that Gallio entered his term of office in the early summer of 51, for there scarcely seems time for him to refer a question to Rome and have the decision back if he was not appointed until 52.[1]

Our difficulties are that, while we know that Paul was in Corinth for eighteen months (Acts 18:11), we do not know at what point in the eighteen months he appeared before the proconsul, nor at what stage of Gallio's proconsulship this took place, nor whether Gallio may, exceptionally, have had a second year in office. The impression left from Acts 18:12–18 is that it was early in Gallio's term of office, and towards the end (though not right at the end) of Paul's eighteen months. If this is so, then Paul arrived in Corinth in the early part of 50, and 1 Thessalonians would have been written soon after,[2] though in view of the uncertainties attaching to the question we can regard this date as approximate only. But it is clear that the letters to the Thessalonians are among the earliest of our New Testament documents. Galatians may have been written earlier, but no other of Paul's letters.[3] The Thessalonian letters must have been written within about twenty years of Jesus' death.

[1] The inscription and other relevant texts are quoted and discussed by Kirsopp Lake in *The Beginnings of Christianity*, v (Baker reprint, 1966), pp. 460–464. Also in George Ogg, *The Chronology of the Life of Paul* (Epworth, 1968), pp. 104–111; J. Murphy-O'Connor, *St. Paul's Corinth* (Glazier, 1983), pp. 141–152.

[2] This date is accepted, among others, by R. H. Fuller, *A Critical Introduction to the New Testament* (Duckworth, 1966), p. 20; G. Bornkamm, *The New Testament, A Guide to its Writings* (SPCK, 1974), p. 92; Everett F. Harrison, *Introduction to the New Testament* (Eerdmans, 1964), p. 249. Others make it a year or two later.

[3] Some scholars, chiefly American, date the letter earlier, say in 45 or 46. But Best seems to have shown that such views are unsatisfactory (Best, pp. 11–13).

III. THE AUTHENTICITY OF 1 THESSALONIANS

The authenticity of 1 Thessalonians has not been seriously doubted other than by the Tübingen school, and the objections they raised have failed to stand the test of time. It is included in Marcion's canon (*c.* AD 140), is mentioned in the Muratorian Fragment (a list of books accepted as Scripture, probably at Rome some time after the middle of the second century), and is quoted by name by Irenaeus (*c.* AD 180), after which it is universally accepted. The contents are all in favour of its being genuine. It is obviously early, for the organization of the church appears to be rudimentary; an answer to the problem of what would happen to those who died before the parousia must have been given early; and it is difficult to imagine a later writer ascribing to Paul after his death statements that might be interpreted to mean that the parousia would occur during his lifetime. The language and ideas are Pauline.

If the letter is not from Paul it is hard to imagine a reason for its composition. There seems no motive for forgery. Indeed, it has been said that the best argument for its authenticity is the letter itself. 'What is its point if it is not a genuine message from the apostle to a Church he has founded and a people whom he loves?'[1] The existence of 2 Thessalonians, whatever its date, seems to imply the existence and acceptance of 1 Thessalonians.[2]

For such reasons as these practically all accept the Epistle as a genuine writing of the apostle. It is sometimes alleged, however, that there are serious discrepancies with Acts, and we must examine these.[3]

1. Paul says that he worked at his trade while in Thessalonica (1 Thes. 2:7–9), which implies a longer period of residence than that covered by the three sabbaths on which he reasoned in the synagogue (Acts 17:2). This is supported by Philippians 4:16, which is held to mean that the Philippians twice sent gifts to Paul while he was at Thessalonica.

[1] Neil, p. xviii.

[2] W. Lock regards this as the 'strongest support' of the authenticity of 1 Thessalonians (HDB, iv. p. 745). So also Plummer I, p. xi.

[3] Of the attitude of some critics Moffatt says, 'It is capricious to pronounce the epistle a colourless imitation, if it agrees with Acts, and unauthentic if it disagrees' (*An Introduction to the Literature of the New Testament* (T. & T. Clark, ³1918), p. 71).

There is no contradiction here. Clearly Paul's visit was in the nature of an evangelistic campaign; he did not have the time to build up the church as he would have wished, so the period must have been short.[1] Even if he was there for only a month it is likely that he would have had to work for his living (not everyone can afford a month without income); and it is not beyond the bounds of possibility, though admittedly not very likely, that within that period the friends from Philippi helped him twice. But the Philippians passage does not necessarily mean that help was sent to Paul twice while he was in Thessalonica. *Hapax kai dis* appears to mean 'more than once', and with *kai* prefixed it will signify, 'both (when I was) in Thessalonica and (*kai*) more than once (*hapax kai dis*) (when I was in other places) you sent . . .'.[2] Even if Acts gives the total duration of the stay there is no contradiction.

But it is not certain that it does. Acts may well be concerned only with the time spent on the Jewish mission; there is nothing in the narrative to exclude a further period among the Gentiles. According to Ramsay the most likely reading of the evidence is that the stay in Thessalonica lasted about six months.[3] This may well be too long, but the point is that the evidence does not support a contradiction.

2. In Acts 17:4 the converts are both Jews and Gentiles, but in Thessalonians there are references to Gentiles (1 Thes. 1:9; 2:14), and the turning from idols points to former pagans rather than to the devout who attached themselves to the synagogues. This, however, shows only that there were various strata among the converts, and that the accounts are independent.

3. Acts 18:5 says that Silas and Timothy rejoined Paul at Corinth, but Thessalonians that Timothy was with Paul in

[1] *Cf.* Lake, 'the suggestion of a more prolonged preaching in Thessalonica seems psychologically as unnecessary as it is certainly historically unvouched for' (*The Earlier Epistles of St. Paul* (Rivingtons, 1911), p. 65). Ward favours a short ministry (p. 8).

[2] Frame (on 1 Thes. 2:18) differs from this view of Phil. 4:16 only in that he understands *hapax kai dis* to mean the slightly stronger 'repeatedly'. See also my note in *Novum Testamentum* 1, 1956, pp. 205–208.

[3] W. M. Ramsay, *St. Paul the Traveller*, p. 228. Findlay thinks that this is 'perhaps, an extreme view' (*CGT*, p. xx, n. 1), but he thinks the duration of the mission to have been months, rather than weeks. Kümmel argues for a lengthy period (*Introduction*, p. 182), and W. Marxsen for a longer period than four weeks (*Introduction to the New Testament* (Fortress, 1974), p. 33).

Athens (1 Thes. 3:1–2). This simply means that neither is giving a full report. Clearly Timothy came to Athens, Paul sent him back to Thessalonica, and in due course, in company with Silas, he rejoined Paul at Corinth. As F. B. Clogg says, 'Discrepancies of this nature prove little except that the authors of Acts and of 1 Thessalonians wrote independently of each other.'[1]

IV. THE PURPOSE OF 1 THESSALONIANS

Some have held that Paul was answering a letter from the Thessalonian believers, the chief points being the following:

1. The apostle's use of 'now about' (4:9, 13; 5:1), which is like the way he introduces answers to points in a letter the Corinthians wrote to him (1 Cor. 7:1, 25; 8:1, *etc.*).

2. Some turns of phrase are held to show that Paul was responding to what the Thessalonians had written, for example, 'we also' (*kai hēmeis*, 2:13), and the repeated 'you know' (1:5; 2:1, 5, 11; 3:3, 4), which are taken as meaning 'as you said'.

3. The way Paul introduces some topics seems to show that he did not really want to deal with them (*e.g.* 4:9; 5:1); the implication is that he is referring to questions asked in a letter.

4. Quick changes of subject show that Paul was going through the points raised in a letter.

Rendel Harris argued the case,[2] and it was accepted by Frame, Lake and others. It is possible, but the evidence is far from conclusive. If Paul had a letter from the Thessalonians, why does he not mention it somewhere (*cf.* 1 Cor. 7:1)? It is better to see Paul as dealing with points made in an oral report by Timothy and Silas.[3] The principal points that called for attention seem to have been the following:

1. The Jewish opponents of the Christian way were maintaining a campaign in which a principal element seems to have been slander of Paul. If they could have succeeded in demonstrating that his conduct was dishonourable they might well have made it very difficult for his converts to hold their ground.

---

[1] F. B. Clogg, *An Introduction to the New Testament* (Hodder and Stoughton, [2]1940), p. 21.
[2] *The Expositor*, Fifth Series, VIII, pp. 168ff.
[3] See further, Hendriksen, pp. 12–13.

They appear to have insinuated that Paul's aim was to make a profit out of them, that he was like some of the wandering teachers of philosophy or religion who abounded at this time. So, too, they apparently made capital out of his failure to return, alleging that it showed him to have no real love for his converts. They probably suggested that there was nothing divine about Paul's message, and that it had originated in the apostle's own fertile mind. Paul is answering allegations of this kind throughout his first three chapters, and the fact that he thought it necessary to devote so much space to the topic may indicate that the whispering campaign was having some measure of success.

2. There was persecution by the pagans (2:14).

3. In a pagan environment pressure was always being exerted on those newly converted to revert to easy-going pagan standards in sexual matters (4:4–8).

4. Some of the Christians had apparently understood Paul to have said that Christ would come back and receive them all to himself. When some of them died they thought this meant that they would lose their share in the glory that would come with the return of Christ (4:13–18).

5. It is possible that some were worried about when Christ's return would take place (5:1–11).

6. Some of the brothers seem to have been content to live off their fellows, instead of earning their own living (4:11–12).

7. A tension may have been present between some of the leading members and the rest of the congregation (5:12–13).

8. There may have been some difficulty about the work of the Holy Spirit and the importance to be attached to spiritual gifts (5:19–20).

Some argue for consistent opposition from one group of opponents, *e.g.* W. Schmithal's view that Gnostics were in mind or R. Jewett's discussion of 'enthusiastic radicals' (see Best, pp. 16–22, for a good summary). But the evidence indicates a variety of opponents and problems.

Much of this is explicable as the difficulties which a young, very enthusiastic, but as yet imperfectly instructed, church would naturally encounter as it sought to live out its faith. We meet the weak and the faint-hearted, the idlers and the workers, the visionaries and the puzzled.

So Paul the pastor wrote to meet the need of his flock. It is clear enough that, on the whole, he was well satisfied with the progress the Thessalonians had made; indeed, the news brought to him had thrilled him. But he was never the man to dwell on past achievements, whether his own or those of his converts. So he applies himself at once to the task of meeting the needs that had become apparent. The result is a moving document; while it is true that many of the important Pauline doctrines are absent, it is also true that the letter shows us something of Paul's pastoral zeal and his intense interest in the spiritual well-being of his converts. Here we catch a glimpse of Paul the man in a way not always obvious when he is taken up with questions of more profound theological significance.

V. THE AUTHENTICITY OF 2 THESSALONIANS

The authenticity of this Epistle is supported by considerations such as the following:

1. This letter is, if anything, better attested than the first. Polycarp, Ignatius and Justin all seem to have known it; it is included in the Marcionite canon and the Muratorian Fragment; Irenaeus quotes it by name. Thereafter it is universally accepted.

2. The vocabulary, style and basic theology are as Pauline as those of 1 Thessalonians.

3. The general situation presupposed and the contents are in agreement with what we might expect if Paul were the author.

4. There seems no suitable alternative. If Paul did not write the letter we must suppose that a forger did. We cannot regard it as a well-intentioned writing under the general coverage of the apostle's name, for it claims to have Paul's authentic signature (2 Thes. 3:17). But what possible motive could a forger have? Unless the letter is written to meet the genuine need of the Thessalonian church there seems no point in it. Nor can we understand why the forger should make it so like 1 Thessalonians, or for that matter how he did it. He must have entered very fully into the apostle's mind.

5. Finally, there is the point (made by von Dobschütz and

others) that the only reason for doubting the authenticity of 2 Thessalonians is that we possess 1 Thessalonians. It is strange to reject an Epistle that contains nothing un-Pauline and bears all the marks of a Pauline writing, simply because another Pauline writing is markedly similar.

Such considerations convince many, but by no means all. Masson, Marxsen and others[1] deny that the letter is Pauline. They adduce arguments such as the following:

1. Eschatology

The eschatology is said to be inconsistent with that of 1 Thessalonians. There, it is urged, Christ's return is imminent and will occur suddenly; in 2 Thessalonians it is to be preceded by signs, notably the appearance of the Man of Lawlessness. But it is difficult to take this argument seriously; it demands a logical consistency that is foreign to the very nature of apocalyptic. Most apocalypses manage to hold to the two ideas of suddenness and of the appearance of preparatory signs. Again, the fact that Paul exhorts his readers not to let Christ's return catch them unprepared (1 Thes. 5:1–11) points to some knowledge of signs preceding it, which is in agreement with 2 Thessalonians.

Some urge that 2 Thessalonians contains a view of the anti-Christ without parallel in the New Testament and therefore we cannot ascribe it to Paul. But this is a palpable *non sequitur*. If it is unique, that is no reason for denying it to Paul. He is just the kind of thinker to come up with an idea that nobody else in the early church could have produced. The suggestion that the teaching on the last things (2 Thes. 2:1–11) is different from that in other Pauline letters is no more convincing. The point is that the problem being dealt with (the assertion that the parousia is past, not imminent) is different from the problem faced elsewhere, so it is not surprising that the solution is different.

Another objection might be put this way. People who needed

---

[1] See, for example, G. Bornkamm, *The New Testament*, p. 93; R. Bultmann, *Theology of the New Testament*, ii (SCM, 1955), p. 142; H. J. Schoeps sees divided opinions, but excludes it from his list of Paul's 'seven certainly genuine letters' (*Paul* (Lutterworth, 1961), pp. 51–52).

instruction in elementary matters (like those dealt with in 1 Thes. 4:13–18) could not possibly have known what 2 Thessalonians presupposes its readers knew about the anti-Christ. But it is fairly retorted that Paul did not have sufficient time while in Thessalonica to give all the teaching on this subject that he would have liked. It is quite possible that some of his converts received enthusiastically his general teaching on the parousia (and thus on the anti-Christ) without getting to grips with the problem of those who had died before the parousia. Indeed, this is a problem that might well have suggested itself only when some of the Thessalonian believers died.

Not many these days argue that the section on the anti-Christ refers to the Nero *redivivus* myth, the expectation that in due course Nero would come back to life again and lead a force opposed to all that is good. The myth did not arise until years after Nero's death in AD 68, so that if this is in mind Paul cannot have been the author. But it is now clear that the idea of the anti-Christ is far older than the concept of Nero *redivivus* and that it goes back to a time before that of Paul. There is no problem here.[1]

The difference in eschatology between the two letters is one of emphasis, not principle. As Clogg puts it: 'It is reasonable to suppose that the Apostle is correcting a misapprehension, or possibly a wilful misapprehension, of the eschatology of the first letter, rather than that he is correcting the eschatology itself.'[2]

2. The combination of likeness and difference

The main argument against the authenticity of this letter is the problem of accounting for the combination of likeness to and

---

[1] *Cf.* F. C. Beare, the theory 'was demolished . . . by the studies of apocalyptic literature made by Gunkel, Bousset, and Charles' (*IDB*, 4, p. 625).

[2] F. B. Clogg, *Introduction*, p. 25. Findlay thinks that, since 2 Thessalonians 'is written on purpose to qualify the former and to correct an erroneous inference that might be drawn from it . . . a *prima facie* disagreement on the point is only to be expected' (*CGT*, p. lii). Writing in 1911, Kirsopp Lake could say: 'the result of the last fifteen years of research is decisively to remove the eschatological argument from the list of possible objections to the authenticity of 2 Thessalonians' (*Earlier Epistles*, p. 80). Despite the work of some recent scholars, this verdict still appears to be the right one.

difference from 1 Thessalonians. On the one hand there is the fact that large sections of the two Epistles are very similar, and that not only in ideas, but in the actual phraseology used.[1] Would a writer of the calibre of Paul repeat himself in this way after such a short interval when writing to the same people? Deliberate imitation by another, rather than a second letter from the same pen, is said to be the explanation. On the other hand there are differences such as those noticed in the previous section. It is difficult to imagine circumstances which would explain this combination of likeness and difference, and thus some feel that it is better to think of 2 Thessalonians as written by someone other than Paul who tried to gain acceptance for it by passing it off as the product of the great apostle.

Of this we might say, in the first place, that some of the resemblances are such that it is very difficult to think of the author being other than Paul. As we have seen already, the style, vocabulary and ideas are all Pauline, and a forger would have to be imbued with the very mind of Paul to have produced such a work. Deliberate imitation is not the only explanation of the linguistic coincidences. A writer often uses much the same language over a period. T. Zahn held that Paul may have refreshed his memory by looking over a copy of 1 Thessalonians, a possibility Neil accepts, as does A. D. McGiffert, though Milligan scouts the idea.[2]

Another explanation arises from the fact that false teachers made their appearance (2 Thes. 2:2). When Paul heard this, what would be more natural than that he should write to confute them, and, writing soon after the first letter, in much the same words?

Again, the extent of the resemblances should not be exaggerated. If we exclude the framework of the Epistles (opening, closing, *etc.*), the resemblances do not occur in more than about one-third. Moreover, passages with .similar wording are used differently in the two letters. For example, the reference to Paul's working with his hands comes early in the first letter and shows his love for his converts (1 Thes. 2:9); in the second it is

---

[1] See the lists in Rigaux, pp. 133–134.

[2] T. Zahn, *Introduction to the New Testament,* i (T. & T. Clark, 1909), n. 6, pp. 249–250; Neil, p. xxiii; McGiffert, *EB*, col. 5045; Milligan, pp. lxxxiv–lxxxv.

late and is the basis of an exhortation to imitate the apostle
(2 Thes. 3:7–9).[1]

We may use the verdict of Lake to sum up this section: 'The
main argument against the Epistle is the difficulty of imagining
circumstances to account for its curious combination of likeness
to and difference from the First Epistle – and such an argument
is too negative to be ever quite decisive.'[2]

3. *Difference in tone*

The general tone of 2 Thessalonians is said to be colder and
more formal than that of the first Epistle. To which, in the first
place, we may well ask why a second letter should precisely
reproduce the tone of the first,[3] especially when the first was
evidently written in a time of exaltation, for Paul was reacting
from extreme discouragement. Indeed, since it is clear that some
of the rebukes given in the first Epistle have to be repeated in
the second, it should not surprise us if a tone of asperity were
to creep in. This is all the more important in that Paul's circumstances seem not to have been happy at the time he wrote the
second letter (2 Thes. 3:2).

But we may well doubt whether the difference in tone is as
pronounced as is alleged. It depends on a few expressions such
as 'We ought always to thank God for you, brothers, and rightly
so' (2 Thes. 1:3, and *cf.* 2:13), 'we command you' (2 Thes. 3:6,
12). There is, however, little that is formal or cold in the way
Paul deals with the offenders. Moreover, most of the colour in
the first Epistle comes in the section where Paul is defending
himself against the slanderers (2:1–13); for the rest, there is not
much difference in tone between the two. As Frame says, 'Omit

---

[1] *Cf.* Frame, 'Apart from the epistolary outline, the agreements are seldom lengthy.
Furthermore, the setting of the phrases in II is usually different from their setting in I'
(p. 49).

[2] K. Lake, *The Earlier Epistles*, p. 86.

[3] 'We are not called upon to assume that Paul at all times lived in the same mood of
emotional exaltation . . . it is unreasonable to expect him always to write in the same key'
(R. H. Walker, *ISBE*, v. p. 2969). Similarly Findlay reports Bornemann's view that, by the
time of 2 Thessalonians, 'St Paul was immersed in Corinthian affairs . . . his heart was no
longer away at Thessalonica as when he first wrote' (*CGT*, p. xlix).

the self-defence from I and the difference in tone between I and II would not be perceptible.'[1]

Thus none of the considerations urged against the authenticity of the Epistle can be held to be decisive. In view of this we should go along with the positive evidence and conclude that this is a genuine Epistle of Paul.[2]

VI. THE RELATION BETWEEN THE TWO EPISTLES

To decide in favour of the authenticity of 2 Thessalonians does not settle the question of the relationship between the two Epistles. A number of suggestions have been put forward.

1. A church in two sections

Harnack thought that the Jews and the Gentiles in the church at Thessalonica were so out of step with each other that they met separately.[3] He thought that 1 Thessalonians is addressed to the Gentile section of the church, and 2 Thessalonians to the Jewish section. He claimed that, whereas the first Epistle seems to have Gentiles in mind (cf. the references to turning to God from idols, 1 Thes. 1:9), there is a marked Jewish colouring in the second, which points to a different public and one familiar with Old Testament phraseology. This, however, does not amount to very much, for Paul's most copious use of the Old Testament is in Romans, addressed, most agree, to a church that was predominantly Gentile.

Moreover, the Jewish tone of 2 Thessalonians is not very clear. There is not one direct quotation from the Old Testament, and Plummer, who has searched both Epistles for traces of LXX phraseology, finds this 'less conspicuous' in the second

---

[1] Frame, p. 35.

[2] A. F. J. Klijn sees no reason to doubt the letter's authenticity: 'The second letter is evidently based on more detailed information concerning certain difficulties for which the first letter could not yet provide an explicit answer' (An Introduction to the New Testament (Brill, 1967), p. 123).

[3] This view attracted Lake (The Earlier Epistles, p. 84; Introduction, p. 134).

than in the first.[1]

A second argument is based on the fact that, where the text usually accepted reads 'from the beginning (*ap' archēs*) God chose you' (2 Thes. 2:13), there is a variant, 'a first-fruit (*aparchēn*)'. The variant has sufficiently strong manuscript support for Lake to say, 'there is about as much to be said for the one reading as the other'.[2] If it be accepted, it supports Harnack's view, for, while the Thessalonians were not in any sense a first-fruit (being neither Paul's first converts, nor the first in Macedonia), the Jewish Christians were the first-fruits of the Thessalonian church.

Then there is the use of 'all' (1 Thes. 5:26–27). It is felt that there must be something behind the insistence that *all* the brothers be greeted, and that the letter be read to *all*.

There seem, however, to be insuperable difficulties in the way of this view.

1. It is incredible that the man who wrote 1 Corinthians 1:11–17 should meekly acquiesce in a situation where a church of his foundation was so hopelessly divided. The idea contradicts his repeated stress on unity.

2. It is difficult to explain Paul's evident pleasure in the Thessalonians if such a split existed.

3. The division of a church into two communities of this kind is so contradictory of all that we know of apostolic Christianity that we could accept it only on the basis of very strong evidence.

4. Even if there was a split church anywhere, the evidence that the church in Thessalonica was so divided is very weak, to put it mildly.

---

[1] Plummer II, pp. xvii–xix. Milligan, however, finds 2 Thes. 1:6–10 the best illustration of his contention that in these two Epistles 'there are whole passages which are little more than a mosaic of O.T. words and expressions' (pp. lviii–lix), while Findlay thinks the mind of the writer of 2 Thessalonians to be 'full of the apocalyptic ideas of the Books of Isaiah and Daniel, to a less extent of Ezekiel and the Psalter' and 'his prophetical and hortatory passages are so steeped in the O.T., beyond what is common with St Paul, that this fact is even urged as evidence for inauthenticity' (p. lx).

[2] K. Lake, *The Earlier Epistles*, p. 84. It is adopted in the 26th edition of the Nestle-Aland *Greek New Testament*. Alfred Wikenhauser objects that 'if it were the correct reading we should expect a genitive after it' (*New Testament Introduction* (Herder, 1958), p. 371). R. V. G. Tasker argues for *ap' archēs* as 'in keeping with Paul's thought' (*The Greek New Testament* (Oxford and Cambridge, 1964), p. 440).

5. The superscriptions of the two Epistles are practically identical, and there is not the slightest indication that they are addressed to different groups. Harnack has to suppose that the words 'which are of the circumcision' have dropped out of the text in the second Epistle.

6. On this hypothesis, a passage intended for the Gentile section of the church (1 Thes. 2:13–16) holds up for admiration the conduct of the churches in Judea and commends the Thessalonians for following this example. We should also notice that there are traces of LXX language behind some of the phraseology of the first Epistle.[1]

7. Each of the points adduced in favour of the hypothesis may fairly be disputed; the more Jewish tone of 2 Thessalonians is difficult to sustain; the variant reading does not carry conviction; the 'all' (1 Thes. 5:26–27) is not particularly emphatic and is accounted for by Paul's desire to send his greetings to everybody (see the commentary, *ad loc.*).

2. *Co-authorship*

Some have felt that the best solution is to think of Silas[2] or Timothy[3] as the real author of one or both Epistles, with Paul simply adding a general authentication. But this really solves nothing. If, with Burkitt, we think of Silas as the author of both Epistles, we are faced with exactly the same problems as when we think of Paul as the author of both. If we take Paul to be the author of the first Epistle and Timothy or Silas to have written the second, we are faced with the problem of the similarities of style and language in the two letters. Nor is the theory any better when it comes to explaining the differences between the

---

[1] Plummer finds evidence of LXX phraseology behind six or seven passages in this Epistle (Plummer I, pp. xx–xxii).

[2] Burkitt thought that both letters 'were drafted by Silvanus-Silas, that they were read to Paul, who approved them and added 1 Thess. ii. 18 and 2 Thess. iii. 17 with his own hand' (quoted in *NBC*, p. 1161). E. G. Selwyn sees Silvanus also as Peter's secretary (*The First Epistle of St. Peter* (Macmillan, 1947), pp. 9–17).

[3] W. Lock cites Spitta as holding this view. He thinks Silas more likely than Timothy, 'but the theory creates more difficulties than it solves' (HDB, iv, p. 748). Milligan examines this view but finds against it 'the want . . . of any satisfactory direct evidence' (p. xc).

two, for Paul clearly signed 2 Thessalonians (2 Thes. 3:17), and we cannot imagine him putting his signature to something with which he disagreed.

3. Reversal of order

We have assumed that 1 Thessalonians was written first and 2 Thessalonians after a short interval, but some scholars have felt that many of the difficulties are solved if we reverse the order. The reason for thinking 2 Thessalonians unauthentic, they suggest, is that we read it in the shadow of 1 Thessalonians, and beside that letter it does appear as something in the nature of a pale copy. But, as a first letter, it is full of life and interest, though it leaves some things unsettled and thus calls for the fuller letter to follow.[1]

The chief arguments for seeing 2 Thessalonians as written first seem to be these:

1. The trials and tribulations are at their height in 2 Thessalonians, but seem past in 1 Thessalonians (cf. 1 Thes. 2:14).

2. In 2 Thessalonians the internal difficulties in the church are spoken of as a new development of which the letter-writers have just heard, whereas in 1 Thessalonians they are referred to as completely familiar to all concerned.

3. The emphasis on the autograph (2 Thes. 3:17) as a mark of genuineness is pointless except in a first letter.

4. The statement that the Thessalonians have no need to be instructed about times and dates (1 Thes. 5:1) is very relevant if they are acquainted with 2 Thessalonians 2. Gregson finds the eschatology of the first Epistle 'more mature' than that of the second.[2]

5. As we saw above (p. 24), there are expressions which might be held to indicate that 1 Thessalonians is the reply to a letter from the church in that city. Manson thinks that the

---

[1] The view goes back to Grotius: 'Grotius thinks that 2 Thess. was written as early as 38 A.D., before Paul visited Thessalonica, to certain Jewish Christians there' (Zahn, Introduction, i, p. 241). See also T. W. Manson, BJRL 35, 1952–53, pp. 438–447; R. Gregson, EQ, 38, 1966, pp. 76–80; J. C. Hurd, IDB, v, p. 901, etc.

[2] R. Gregson, art. cit., p. 77.

answers may well be to certain questions arising from what Paul says in 2 Thessalonians.[1]

6. 1 Thessalonians precedes 2 Thessalonians in our Bibles only because it is longer.[2]

7. When Timothy was sent to Thessalonica (1 Thes. 3:2) he would have taken a letter with him. If not 2 Thessalonians, where is it?

8. 2 Thessalonians says nothing about Paul's proposed visit (1 Thes. 2:18). The desire was formed after 2 Thessalonians was written.

9. Wherever the two letters have common material, 1 Thessalonians is fuller and has new material.

None of these is really convincing. It is by no means clear from 1 Thessalonians that the trials are over (*cf.* 1 Thes. 3:3) and, indeed, most students have felt that part, at least, of the purpose of that Epistle is to encourage the readers in view of the difficulties ahead. The idea that the internal difficulties mentioned are a new development in 2 Thessalonians seems to rest on the words, 'We hear that some . . .' (2 Thes. 3:11); but this is just as compatible with a report reaching Paul after 1 Thessalonians as before it. Otherwise the injunctions in the second letter are very similar to those in the first. That an autograph is likely in a first letter is negated by the fact that it is not usual in the Pauline correspondence.[3] Its occurrence here seems to be due to special circumstances (2 Thes. 2:2). The eschatological argument is unconvincing and could support the priority of either letter. The use of 'Now about . . .' is no proof of a letter; it could well refer to matters mentioned by Timothy in his verbal report to Paul. The canonical order proves nothing one way or the other. Timothy was co-author of 2 Thessalonians, which makes it unlikely that he would have been its bearer. The absence of a reference to Paul's desire to visit the church in

---

[1] T. W. Manson, *art. cit.*, pp. 443–444. But 'it is not difficult to construct a series of questions to which portions of 1 Thessalonians might be an answer. A similar letter of inquiry might be constructed to fit Philippians, but it would go very little way towards proving that any such letter had been written' (Plummer I, pp. xviii–xix).

[2] But this is the order in the canon of the second-century heretic Marcion, which apparently preceded the rule about length and appears to be based on chronological order.

[3] The autograph occurs in 1 Cor. 16:21 (though 1 Cor. 5:9 shows this to be a second letter); Col. 4:18; but no attention is drawn to it in either case, as is done in 2 Thes. 3:17.

2 Thessalonians proves nothing. An abbreviated reference to earlier matter is just as likely as the introduction of new material. In any case the treatment of the idlers is fuller in the second letter than the first. D. Guthrie is justified in saying, 'none of these reasons is convincing taken separately, nor is the cumulative effect any more so'.[1]

Against the position we may note some points:

1. Each of the problems occupying Paul's attention – persecution, the parousia, idleness – seems to intensify and deepen as we pass from the first Epistle to the second.

2. There are passages in 2 Thessalonians that refer to a letter (2:2, 15; 3:17). Unless we take these to refer to 1 Thessalonians, we must posit some lost Epistle.

3. The personal reminiscences that form so prominent a part of the first letter are lacking in the second, which is perfectly natural if the latter is something of a sequel to the first, but not so natural in a first letter. So conclusive did this seem to Milligan, that he could say that the idea of the priority of 2 Thessalonians 'is excluded by I. ii. 17–iii. 6 which could hardly have been written by St Paul, if he had previously addressed a letter to Thessalonica'.[2]

4. We have seen that the warmth of the expressions in the first letter springs naturally out of the news that Timothy brought, while the slightly cooler tone of 2 Thessalonians is natural later on. It is difficult to reverse the situation.

5. There is no definite proposal for a visit in 1 Thessalonians 2:17–19, but only longing. This could take place at any time.

Thus the balance of evidence seems to indicate that the usual order of these letters is the right one. Best makes the interesting point that no-one who has written a commentary on 2 Thessalonians holds that it was written first.[3]

---

[1] D. Guthrie, *New Testament Introduction* (Inter-Varsity Press, 1970), p. 577.

[2] Milligan, p. xxxix. *Cf.* B. Jowett: 'It is improbable (observe, however, 2 Thess. ii. 15) that a previous Epistle could have interposed itself between the visit of the Apostle and chapters two and three of the First Epistle. (Compare Acts xvii, xviii.)' (Jowett, p. 67).

[3] Best, p. 45.

VII. THE OCCASION AND PURPOSE OF 2 THESSALONIANS

The position, then, would seem to be that Paul wrote 1 Thessalonians, but that it did not achieve all that he desired. Further reports reaching him showed that his defence of his own conduct had proved adequate (he apparently had no need to speak further about this), but apparently other parts of his letter were not so effective. Idleness on the part of some continued, and there were misunderstandings about the parousia which caused others to be troubled in mind. Accordingly, without losing time (by common consent there cannot have been more than a matter of weeks between the two Epistles), Paul set himself the task of putting things in order, and 2 Thessalonians was the result. It must have been written soon after 1 Thessalonians, because it must have been sent before Paul's second visit to Thessalonica (see Acts 20:1–2), and Corinth is the only place known to us where Paul, Silas and Timothy were together during the intervening period.

In this letter he carries on the work he began in the first, encouraging the faint-hearted, rebuking the slackers, dealing again with the return of the Lord. 'It is simply a second prescription for the same case, made after discovering that some certain stubborn symptoms had not yielded to the first treatment.'[1]

[1] R. H. Walker, *ISBE*, v, p. 2968.

1 THESSALONIANS: ANALYSIS

I. GREETING (1:1)

II. PRAYER OF THANKSGIVING (1:2–3)

III. REMINISCENCES OF THESSALONICA (1:4 – 2:16)
   a. *Response of the Thessalonians* (1:4–10)
   b. *The preaching of the gospel at Thessalonica* (2:1–16)
      1. *The preachers' motives* (2:1–6)
      2. *The preachers' maintenance* (2:7–9)
      3. *The preachers' behaviour* (2:10–12)
      4. *The preachers' message* (2:13)
      5. *Persecution* (2:14–16)

IV. THE RELATIONSHIP OF PAUL TO THE THESSALONIANS (2:17 – 3:13)
   a. *Paul's desire to return* (2:17–18)
   b. *Paul's joy* (2:19–20)
   c. *Timothy's mission* (3:1–5)
   d. *Timothy's report* (3:6–8)
   e. *Paul's satisfaction* (3:9–10)
   f. *Paul's prayer* (3:11–13)

V. EXHORTATION TO CHRISTIAN LIVING (4:1–12)
   a. *General* (4:1–2)
   b. *Sexual purity* (4:3–8)
   c. *Brotherly love* (4:9–10)
   d. *Earning one's living* (4:11–12)

1 THESSALONIANS: COMMENTARY

I. GREETING (1:1)

Letters in antiquity began with some variant of the formula 'A to B greeting', usually followed by some pious expression such as a prayer. This was just as much part of the letter as our 'Dear Sir' at the beginning and 'Yours faithfully' or 'Yours sincerely' at the end (though we may be addressing an enemy, and be neither faithful nor sincere). Here is an example of the beginning of an actual letter:

> Antonis Longus to Nilus his mother many greetings. And continually do I pray that thou art in health. I make intercession for thee day by day to the lord Serapis.[1]

After this preamble the writer begins his message. Paul used the conventional opening, varying it according to circumstances; but in his hands it took on a characteristically Christian shape.

1. Here Paul associates Silvanus and Timothy (see Introduction, pp. 17–18) with himself, but there seems little doubt that the body of the letter is from Paul. It bears the marks of his style and gives no appearance of being composite. In all his letters, except those to the Thessalonians, Philippians and Philemon, he asserts his apostleship; its absence here may point to the amicable relations between Paul and this church.

Though this is the shortest of the extant superscriptions it contains all the elements that appear in the fully developed

---

[1] A. Deissmann, *LAE*, p. 188.

form: the address to the church, the linking of the church with the Father and the Son, and the prayer for grace and peace. The address, *To the church of the Thessalonians*, is a form found only in these Epistles, though it is not unlike that in Galatians, another early Epistle. Paul may be thinking of the local gathering of believers, rather than of the church as the local expression of the church universal as in the later letters (so Milligan).

Also peculiar to these Epistles is the phrase *in God the Father and the Lord Jesus Christ* (Paul usually says 'in Christ'). It is striking (a) that he speaks of *the Father* and *the Lord* in one breath (no-one else could be linked with *the Father* in this way), (b) that he joins the two under one preposition *in*, and (c) that he expresses the closeness of the tie linking the Thessalonians with their God in terms of Christ as well as the Father. 'The association could hardly be closer' (Ward). This high view of Jesus is continued with the use of *Lord* and *Christ*. *Lord* was used in LXX as the translation of the divine name and it was commonly used of deity in other religions (as well as having less significant uses). It points to a very high place. *Christ* means 'anointed' and is equivalent to 'Messiah'. And all this in a letter written only about twenty years after the crucifixion. From very early times Jesus was seen to have the highest place.

The greeting *Grace and peace to you* looks like a combination of the usual Greek and Hebrew forms, with a slight but significant change in the Greek, from *chairein* ('greeting') to *charis* ('grace'). *Grace* is one of the great Christian words. Cognate with *chara* ('joy'), it means basically 'that which causes joy'. In a Christian context nothing brings joy like the act of God in Christ whereby sin is put away and salvation is made available as a free gift. The word comes then to mean any free gift of God, and in greetings it is used in this general sense, though with a glance at God's great gift to mankind.

With us *peace* is a negative concept, the absence of war. But the Hebrew equivalent, *shalôm*, is concerned with 'wholeness', 'soundness', and signifies prosperity in the widest sense, especially prosperity in spiritual things. When the Old Testament was translated into Greek, *shalôm* was rendered by *eirēnē* (the word used here), and thus, for those steeped in the Old Testament, *peace* is this broad concept of the prosperity of the whole man, more especially his spiritual prosperity. But 'peace of heart' (LB; 'heart peace', Amp.) misses the point that it is the prosperity of the whole man that is in mind.

There may be significance in the invariable order of these two words in greetings: first *grace*, then *peace*. There can be no true peace until the grace of God has dealt with sin.

The words 'from God our Father, and the Lord Jesus Christ' (AV, LB) are not in the oldest MSS and should not be read.

II. PRAYER OF THANKSGIVING (1:2-3)

We should not take Paul's thanksgiving as merely conventional; he omits it where it does not apply (*e.g.* Galatians; *cf.* Schlier).

2. The writers *always thank God* for these converts, and do so for *all* of them; apparently there were no disaffected members. Like the Philippians, the Thessalonians seem to have been a continual joy to Paul.

3. Paul gives thanks for the faith, hope and love manifest among the Thessalonians, three qualities that are linked a number of times by early Christians (Rom. 5:2-5; 1 Cor. 13:13; Gal. 5:5-6; Col. 1:4-5; Heb. 6:10-12; 10:22-24; 1 Pet. 1:21-22).

The first point is *your work produced by faith*. When Paul is emphasizing that salvation comes from faith and not at all from works, he can set faith and works in sharp contrast; thus we are 'justified by faith in Christ and not by observing the law, because by observing the law no-one will be justified' (Gal. 2:16). But while Paul insists that salvation is all of God, he also insists that faith is busy. Elsewhere he speaks of 'faith working through love' (Gal. 5:6, RSV), and here of faith leading to work. When he speaks of their *labour prompted by love* Paul means more than small deeds of kindness done without hope of reward. The word *kopos* denotes laborious toil, unceasing hardship borne for love's sake.

Love is our translation of *agapē*, a word not used much before the Christians took it up and made it their characteristic word for love. They had not only a new word but a new idea, an idea we see in the love shown in Christ's death for sinners (Jn. 3:16; Rom. 5:8; 1 Jn. 4:10, *etc*.). 'Perhaps as good a way as any of grasping the new idea of love the Christians had is to contrast it with the idea conveyed by *erōs* . . . *erōs* has two principal characteristics: it is a love of the worthy and it is a love that desires to possess. *Agapē* is in contrast at both points: it is not a love of the worthy, and it is not a love that desires to possess. On the contrary, it is a love given quite irrespective of merit, and it is a love that seeks to give.'[1] God loves, not because people are worthy of that love, but because he is that kind of God; it is his nature to love, he *is* love (1 Jn. 4:8, 16).

When this love comes to us we are faced with a challenge we cannot ignore. Once we see that God is like that, that God loves as part of his very nature, that God loves in a way that means Calvary, we must make a decision. Either we yield to the divine *agapē* to be transformed by it, to be re-made in the divine image, to see people in a measure as God sees them, or we do not. And if we do not, in that lies our condemnation. We have shut ourselves up to lovelessness. But those who yield themselves to God are transformed by the power of the divine *agapē*, so that they rejoice to give themselves in the service of others. Paul thanks God that this is what the Thessalonians have done.

The third cause for thanksgiving is their *endurance inspired by hope in our Lord Jesus Christ*, and again this must be understood carefully. *Hypomonē*, rendered *endurance*, means not a negative, passive acquiescence, but an active, manly endurance: 'not the resignation of the passive sufferer, so much as the fortitude of the stout-hearted soldier' (*CBSC*; see also 2 Thes. 3:5). *Hope*, in a Christian context, always has an air of certainty about it. It is a confident expectation, not the unfounded optimism we often mean by the word. More particularly, the Christian hope is directed towards the second advent which seems to be in mind here (so Findlay, Milligan, Masson, *etc*.). Alternatively it is grammatically possible to take the words *in our Lord Jesus Christ*

---

[1] Leon Morris, *Testaments of Love* (Eerdmans, 1981), p. 128. See also A. Nygren, *Agape and Eros* (SPCK, 1953); C. Spicq, *Agape in the New Testament* (St. Louis and London, 1966); C. S. Lewis, *The Four Loves* (Bles, 1960).

to refer to all the preceding part of the verse, in which case the whole of the Christian life is said to be lived in Christ (so Neil, JB).

The addition *before our God and Father* (these words come last in the Greek) draws attention to Fatherhood as the essence of the Christian view of God. It also links the Father and the Son in the most intimate way.

III. REMINISCENCES (1:4 – 2:16)

A. RESPONSE OF THE THESSALONIANS (1:4–10)

4. In these two Epistles Paul uses the address *brothers* twenty-one times (and 'brother' another seven times); the tie that bound the proud Pharisee to despised Gentiles was a close one. Barriers insurmountable to men were done away in Christ. In the Greek *loved* is a perfect participle, combining the thoughts that love existed in the past and that it continues into the present in full force. The construction occurs only here in the New Testament (though 2 Thes. 2:13; Jude 1 are similar), and is richer in meaning than the usual expression (found for example in Rom. 1:7). In view of many loose modern ideas about 'the brotherhood of man' it is worth noticing that the New Testament concept of brotherhood is that of a brotherhood of believers. Here it is linked with being loved by God and with election. Both are significant.

Paul speaks of knowing that God *has chosen* them (literally, 'your election'). In the Old Testament God's choice is usually associated with the nation, in the New with individuals. The thought that God has chosen us is another reminder that our salvation is all of God, and not at all due to any effort of our own. In the face of those who hold that election is harsh and arbitrary Paul's reminder that it proceeds from God's love is timely. The reason he knows the Thessalonians to be elect appears to be given in verse 5. Poole comments, 'We cannot know election as in God's secret decree, but as made manifest in the fruits and effects of it.'

5. The reason Paul is sure of the election of the Thessalonians is the effect on them of what he calls *our gospel*. The term points to the content of the original preaching, the good news of God's action to bring salvation to sinners. The possessive *our* may mean that apostles, just as much as other people, need the gospel, or, more probably, that they had made the gospel they preached their own. It was for them far more than a fine theory; it was something to be lived and proclaimed with power. That the gospel *came* may imply that it possesses a vital force; but eloquence is not the explanation of its effectiveness, for it *came to you not simply with words, but also with power* (*cf.* Rom. 1:16, where Anders Nygren comments, 'The gospel is not the presentation of an idea, but the operation of a power'[1]). This power is linked with *the Holy Spirit* (always the source of the Christian's power, *cf.* 1 Cor. 2:4), *and with deep conviction*; the two are closely linked (there is no repetition of *en* in the Greek), which directs us to the inward assurance that the 'powerful operation of the Spirit' (G. Shrenk, *TDNT*, iv, p. 179) had given to both the apostles and their converts. The Spirit was active in both. Some hold that it is not the inward assurance that is in mind, but what G. Delling calls 'great "fulness of divine working"' (*TDNT*, vi, p. 311; so Rigaux); but *deep conviction* seems to be the meaning (with BAGD, Best, *etc.*). GNB adds 'of its truth', but this is not in the Greek and is not necessary.

6. The converts had followed the example of their mentors; they had become *imitators* of the preachers and, because the preachers modelled themselves on Christ (*cf.* 1 Cor. 11:1), *of the Lord*. Notice the conjunction of *severe suffering* and *the joy given by the Holy Spirit*. Affliction has always been the lot of the true disciple of Christ, as he himself foretold (Jn. 16:33). Luther asked reasonably, 'If Christ wore a crown of thorns, why should His followers expect only a crown of roses?' (cited in Neil). But, just as it is true that the Christian will find trouble in the world, so it is true that he will have a joy that the world never gave and can never take away (Jn. 16:22), a joy brought by the Holy Spirit (Gal. 5:22).

---

[1] A. Nygren, *Commentary on Romans* (SCM, 1952), p. 67.

7–8. Paul has appealed to the example set by the apostles (v. 5) and he proceeds to point out that the converts in their turn had become an example to others. The word *typos*, translated *a model*, meant originally the mark of a stroke or blow (the 'mark' of Jn. 20:25), then a figure formed by a blow, an impression left by a seal or die, an image generally (Acts 7:43), and so it came to mean a pattern (Heb. 8:5), which is its meaning here. This is high praise, for in the first place Paul calls no other church a pattern, and in the second he thinks of the Thessalonians as an example, not only to the heathen, but also to Christians throughout Greece. Indeed, their reputation is world-wide. Paul's *from you* is emphatic (they were special), and his *rang out* (*exēcheō*) is picturesque; it might describe the clarion call of a trumpet or the roll of thunder. It emphasizes the resounding nature of the witness borne by the Thessalonian church. The verb is a Greek perfect, which implies that the sounding out was continuing. It was no passing whim.

The Lord's message (RSV 'the word of the Lord') is an expression very common in the prophetic writings of the Old Testament and found often in Acts, but twice only (here and 2 Thes. 3:1) in Paul (though it is not very different from expressions such as 'the word', 'the word of God', 'the gospel of God' and the like, which are frequent in Paul). It emphasizes the conviction of the early Christians that the message they proclaimed was not the product of human wisdom, but truly of divine origin. This message is said to have sounded out *in Macedonia and Achaia*, the two provinces which together embraced all Greece (Rigaux points out that Paul usually refers to provinces rather than to cities). Paul adds that the faith of the Thessalonians *has become known everywhere*. This may be a hyperbole; but it may also reflect the fact that Aquila and Priscilla had come to Corinth from Rome just before Paul wrote this letter (Acts 18:2), and what was known at Rome could be presumed to be known everywhere.

The sentence looks as though it should end at *everywhere*, but it is typical of Paul's impetuous style that he should go off on a new tack. So he adds that the faith of the Thessalonians was so universally spoken of that he himself had no need to say anything about it.

9. *They themselves* is sometimes taken to indicate people from Macedonia and Achaia, but is probably quite general. Anyone at all might be found telling of what was going on in Thessalonica (*cf*. Moffatt, 'People tell us of their own accord about the visit we paid to you'). It is not usual in such a context to speak of an 'entering in'[1] (*eisodos*; NIV *reception*), but the term is not difficult to understand. The indirect interrogative *what kind of* points to the success of the visit, a success evident from the following statements.

Paul goes on to describe the conversion of the Thessalonians, and since much of the characteristic Pauline terminology is lacking (*e.g.* justification by faith), it would seem that he is using accepted mission terminology. It seems reasonably clear that the first Christian preachers had a common understanding of the essence of their message and of its effects. Paul is using the recognized vocabulary and he seizes on three main points.

First, they had *turned to God from idols* (which shows that the church was predominantly Gentile); in the first century this was a very important evidence of true conversion. Indeed, in every age it is a mark of the true Christian that he has turned from contemporary idols.

Secondly, they had come to *serve the living and true God*. A negative attitude is not enough. The word rendered *serve* basically means 'serve as a slave' and reminds us of the way Paul delighted to call himself a 'slave of Jesus Christ'. It underlines the whole-hearted nature of Christian service. Notice that God is spoken of as *living*, which contrasts with dead idols ('Only the living God is God', Masson), and *true*, which means 'genuine', used 'Of God in contrast to other gods, who are not *real*' (BAGD). The conjunction of these two terms gives emphatic expression to Paul's essential monotheism.

10. Thirdly, they awaited the second advent. The word *wait for* (*anamenein*, here only in the New Testament) means 'wait expectantly' (NEB; *cf*. Hendriksen, 'to look forward to with patience and confidence'). This is the one place in the Thessa-

---

[1] Deissmann, however, cites an example in a Latin letter of the second century AD (*LAE*, pp. 197–199).

lonian Epistles where Christ is called *Son*; the title is used elsewhere in Paul, but its connection here with the second advent is 'unique' (Best). For Paul the parousia is very important and its neglect in many quarters today is a great loss; its rediscovery is sorely needed, for, as J. E. Fison says, 'it is precisely that kind of conversion which the church as well as the world needs to-day, and which only the rediscovery of a living eschatological hope can produce'.[1]

T. F. Glasson maintains that this is one of the first references to the second advent. He holds that it was not found in the teaching of Jesus and, indeed, does not appear until the Thessalonian letters. He thinks it originated in the early church's study of the Old Testament. Then when the Emperor Caligula attempted to place an image of himself in the temple at Jerusalem, this was interpreted as showing that 'the spirit of Antichrist was abroad', and 'the end of the age was near'.[2] But this reconstruction is not in agreement with much that is said in the Gospels, with early statements like those in Acts 1:11; 3:20–21; 10:42; with the implications of the Aramaic expression *maranatha* (1 Cor. 16:22; it probably means 'Our Lord, come!'), or with the way in which eschatology is integral to the whole gospel. The final consummation is implied in the facts that the old has passed away, that in the coming of the Messiah the new age has dawned, and that the power of God is at work. 'This Act of God must reach its climax in Judgment, in the vindication of the just, and in the supreme, and final, and visible Victory of the Lord' (Neil).

At the same time we must query Neil's further idea that we should see here a timeless truth: 'The Lord is always at hand and comes to every generation, and we pass the Judgment of Doomsday upon ourselves every living moment.' While there is a valuable truth in this, it is not what the New Testament means when it speaks of the second advent, nor in particular what Paul means in this verse. Throughout the New Testament it is clear that the advent referred to is an event that will bring

---

[1] J. E. Fison, *The Christian Hope* (Longmans, 1954), p. 80.
[2] T. F. Glasson, *The Second Advent* (Epworth, 1947), pp. 182, 184. *Cf.* also J. A. T. Robinson, *Jesus and His Coming* (SCM, 1957).

this world as we know it to a decisive close. It is the consummation of the age, and it is difficult to see how we can do without the idea of this consummation. Jesus is to come *from heaven*, the word being plural in the Greek, from which some have seen in it the rabbinic idea of a plurality of heavens (*cf.* 2 Cor. 12:2). But singular and plural are interchanged so much in the New Testament that it is unwise to emphasize the use of the plural.

Paul goes on to refer to Jesus' resurrection. It is a mark of the centrality of this event that even when Paul is thinking of the second coming he refers to Christ as the One *whom he raised from the dead*. The New Testament writers, of course, habitually ascribe the work of the resurrection to the Father. It is the mark of his vindication and approval of the atoning work of the Son.

Paul glances at the humanity of the Saviour with the use of the human name *Jesus*, and says that he *rescues* ('a timeless participle', Frame) *us*. The verb puts emphasis on the greatness of the peril and on the power of him who delivers us. The completeness of the deliverance is underlined by the use of the preposition *ek*; we are delivered right 'out of' the wrath.

The coming wrath is the eschatological wrath, the wrath that will come on evil at the end time. C. H. Dodd and others have made a determined attempt to eliminate the idea of 'the wrath of God' from the Bible by arguing that in Scripture this is no more than a name for an impersonal process; people sin, disaster follows (*cf.* JB, 'retribution'). But it is difficult to substantiate this. It is true that there are some passages, like this one, where the wrath is not explicitly linked with God. But can it be seriously argued that Paul is thinking here of a wrath that is not God's? In any case wrath is explicitly linked with God in a number of passages (*e.g.* Jn. 3:36; Rom. 1:18; 9:22; Eph. 5:6; Col. 3:6; Rev. 11:18; 14:10, 19; 19:15), and the idea is often present when the word 'wrath' is not used (*e.g.* 2 Thes. 1:7–9). Further, the New Testament writers always regard the universe as God's universe. If retribution follows upon sin, then it seems impossible to hold that this takes place independently of God. If we were to maintain this, we would be building up a picture of a God who is personally indifferent to sin. The concept of the wrath of God is a healthy corrective to such unmoral views of

49

the Deity, and it stands as a striking reminder that God is totally opposed to every form of evil.[1]

B. THE PREACHING OF THE GOSPEL AT THESSALONICA
(2:1–16)

Paul proceeds to defend his conduct when at Thessalonica, with the Jewish slanders very much in mind. Rolston finds this 'one of the richest descriptions of the work of a Christian minister to be found in the New Testament'.

1. The preachers' motives (2:1–6)

1. NIV omits Paul's 'For', but the conjunction shows that what follows is a consequence of the preceding (cf. Lightfoot).[2] *You* is emphatic; Wilson speaks of 'this brilliant stroke', in that Paul begins by calling the Thessalonians themselves to witness. They know what had happened. There are further links with 1:9, the unusual word *eisodos* being repeated (there translated 'reception', here *visit*; Schlier sees it as having an active sense as in 1:9, an entrance with the fullness of power), while *you* corresponds to 'they themselves'. What other people reported about the Thessalonians they themselves knew to be true. This opening shows Paul's confidence in his converts, and it also directs their attention to facts within their own knowledge that would refute the accusations of Paul's opponents. If the result of his preaching was so manifest and so definite, then clearly he could not have been the time-server he was now accused of being.

In a masterly understatement Paul goes on to say that his entrance *was not a failure*. The perfect tense of his verb gives the

---

[1] See further my *The Apostolic Preaching of the Cross* (Tyndale, ³1965), chs. V, VI.

[2] There is a marked tendency to omit 'for' (*gar*) in modern translations. The conjunction occurs 23 times in 1 Thessalonians and it is omitted in NIV 10 times, GNB 16 times, JB 17 times, NEB 11 times. By contrast RSV omits only once and NASB not at all. It is true that *gar* may sometimes be legitimately omitted in translation (cf. BDF 452 (1)), but the widespread tendency in modern translations goes too far. Paul has the habit of indicating connections in his thought with this causal conjunction, but the modern practice prevents the reader from following him and obscures a Pauline distinctive. Paul uses *gar* 454 times, which is about 44% of the New Testament total (next highest is Matthew with 124, a long way back). See also Ward's note *ad loc.*

idea of a continuing result: not only did the preaching have immediate impressive consequences, but a permanent change was wrought in the lives of the believers. The word *kenos* (*a failure*) means 'empty'; Paul strongly repudiates any thought that he had frittered his time away in aimless pursuits. He had come with a definite aim, and he had secured what he had aimed at.

2. 'But' (which NIV omits) is *alla*, the strong adversative; the following words are in emphatic contrast to the preceding. Far from the visit being 'a failure', Paul and his companions were bold in their preaching of the gospel. Just before the little band first came to the city they had had to endure physical suffering and mental distress. At Philippi the preachers had undergone the painful punishments of scourging and having their feet fastened in the stocks. Neil thinks that the Pauline correspondence as a whole (and 2 Cor. 11:23ff. in particular) shows that Paul may have been specially sensitive to bodily pain, so that he recalled it with something akin to horror. If this is so, then his fortitude in the face of continual ill-treatment is something to marvel at, and indicates courage of the very highest order. But he remembers not only the physical pain but also the indignities that had been heaped on the Roman citizen at Philippi. *Insulted* (*hybristhentes*) indicates an attitude of haughty insolence on the part of the oppressors (NEB 'outrage').

Despite these troubles the apostolic band had preached boldly. The verb translated *we dared* derives from two words that mean 'all speech'; it points to feeling completely at home so that words flow freely. This includes being without fear and having complete confidence. It is difficult to find one English word that will express both these ideas, so that translations tend to choose one and leave the other (though here Moffatt renders 'we took courage and confidence in our God'). In the New Testament the verb is always connected with Christian preaching. This is done *with the help of our God* (more literally, 'in our God'; 'our God' is characteristic of these two Epistles). Paul is not speaking of merely natural courage, but of the supernatural endowment with which God equips those who put their trust in him.

In this confidence and courage they had proclaimed 'the gospel of God' (so, rather than *his gospel*). In 1:5 it is 'our gospel', for the preachers were proclaiming something they knew for themselves and had made their very own. Here what is singled out for attention is that the gospel is not of human origin. It is nothing less than God's plan for man's salvation. The Christian faith is not the accumulated wisdom of pious souls, nor the insight of men of religious genius, but the divine plan for dealing with our sin.

But at Thessalonica, as at Philippi, there had been *strong opposition*. Rigaux thinks that the word *agōn* here signifies inner tension and Frame that inward trouble may be meant (though he does not commit himself). But the word (which is used of a contest in the Olympic Games) is much more likely to point to acts of opposition, since Paul is speaking of things that might have made him afraid. It is that in Paul's experiences that corresponds to the troubles of the Thessalonians (1:6).

3. Paul's insistence on the purity of the *motives* of the preachers seems to indicate that he is meeting an accusation that their interest was not in their message, but in their profits (like the many itinerant preachers of strange cults and philosophies). *The appeal we make* is the manner of the preaching, as 'the gospel of God' in the previous verse was the matter.

Paul makes three points. First, the preaching was not *from error*; the preachers were not wrong (how could the gospel 'of God' be a mistake?). Secondly, it was not from *impure motives*, which implies that the preachers had been accused of immorality. This may be general (Best), or, more probably, sexual; religious prostitution was characteristic of many of the cults of the day and it seems that Paul was being accused of gross sensuality. Thirdly, the preachers were not *trying to trick* the converts. The word points to cunning craft: it properly signified catching fish with a bait, and thence it came to mean any crafty design for deceiving or catching. There is an interesting change of preposition from 'of' (*ek*, denoting origin) with the first two words to 'in' (*en*) with the last. Paul is saying that his preaching did not spring out of delusion or impurity, nor was it conducted in an atmosphere of craft.

4. The apostle vigorously repudiates these slanders and emphasizes the solemnity of his commission. So far from seeking anything for himself, he could speak only because he was *approved by God to be entrusted with the gospel*. His own subservient position is brought out in this expression, as is the transcendent nature of his message. It came from God and therefore the accusation that he spoke from error was false. The verb *approved* means first 'to test' and then to approve as the result of the test, and the perfect tense used here conveys the meaning that the approval continues. Paul thinks of himself as having been tried out by God, and then trusted for service. It is out of this situation that he and his companions speak, the present tense in the verb *we speak* showing this to be their habitual practice.

Paul is emphatic that the message originated with God; it is not something thought up *to please men*. The word *please* probably means more than the English term suggests. The Greek word can convey the idea of service in the interest of others (MM give examples from the inscriptions). The point is that, while Paul served men, he did not live to serve them. His service was primarily the service of God, and he delighted to refer to himself as 'the slave of God' or 'of Christ'. In every age this needs emphasis, for the Christian preacher is always tempted to accommodate his message to the desires of his hearers. People do not want a message that tells them that they are helpless sinners and that they must depend humbly on God's mercy for their salvation. They are more interested in the 'social implications' of the gospel. These, of course, must not be soft-pedalled, but the preacher must always put his emphasis on those doctrines to which Scripture itself gives priority.

That God *tests our hearts* means that the preacher must be completely sincere. The verb *tests* is that translated *approved* earlier in the verse; it signifies 'put to the test' and thus 'approve by test'. In the Bible 'heart' means the sum total of our inward dispositions, including the emotions, the intellect and the will; it is not confined to the emotions, as usually with us. Paul is saying that the whole of the motives and thoughts of the preacher are always open to God and, further, that his own preaching had been done in the full consciousness of this fact. It is not unlike calling God to witness his sincerity, as he does in the next verse.

5. Paul turns from the general to the particular and from the positive to the negative. There had been three things from which the preaching at Thessalonica had been free. The first is *flattery* (more literally, 'neither have we come to be in a word of flattery'). The verb conveys the idea of entering into and continuing in a given condition (as in Rom. 16:7, of Andronicus and Junia coming to be and continuing to be in Christ). 'In a word' refers to the totality of the preaching, but the remaining word *kolakeias* is difficult to convey exactly in English. It is not flattery in the sense of fair, but insincere, words. Rather it denotes something like 'cajolery' ('deception by slick eloquence', Moore), the use of acceptable speech with the purpose of lulling someone into a sense of security, so that one may obtain one's own ends. Paul emphatically rejects the idea.

He further denies putting on *a mask to cover up greed*. The preachers did not hide their real motives in order to secure personal profit. Some translations concentrate on the money angle (JB 'trying to get money'; LB 'so that you would give us money'), but the word *pleonexia* denotes the general attitude of eager seeking to have more. While it is often shown in the desire for money, it is the spirit of desire in its most general sense, self-aggrandisement. In disavowing any such motive Paul solemnly calls God to witness (*cf*. v. 10; Rom. 1:9; 2 Cor. 1:23; Phil. 1:8). Earlier in the verse he appealed to the Thessalonians' knowledge of the outward (*you know*), here to God's knowledge of the inward.

6. Paul's third disclaimer is that of seeking *praise from men*, whether the Thessalonians or any others. This is a repetition of what has already been said in verse 4, with this difference that there he was denying that he directed his preaching to serve the ends that men approved, whereas now he is thinking of his own inner state; he was not looking for the satisfaction that comes when one's work is praised. Paul did obtain honour, and to this day is honoured by millions throughout the world. But he tells us that he was not looking for this and it is this purity of motive that makes him a worthy object of the praise that

Christians have delighted to lavish on him.

2. The preachers' maintenance (2:7–9)

7. An *apostle* is 'one who is sent', 'a messenger', and the term was in common use among both Jews and pagans. The Jews used the term to denote a man's personal representative, and the Talmud says more than once, 'A man's *shaliach* is as it were himself' (*shaliach* is the Hebrew equivalent of the Greek *apostolos*, 'apostle').[1] For the Christians we see the essence of apostleship in the commission Jesus gave to the Twelve: 'He appointed twelve – designating them apostles – that they might be with him and that he might send them out to preach and to have authority to drive out demons' (Mk. 3:14–15). The essential task of the apostle was to witness to (Acts 1:22) and to proclaim the saving act of God in the gospel. There were other things apostles did, like the organization of new churches, the provision of a ministry for them, and the exercise of oversight. But such things were secondary. Paul could regard the proclamation of the authentic gospel as so much the work of the apostle that he could say, 'even if we or an angel from heaven should preach a gospel other than the one we preached to you, let him be eternally condemned!' (Gal. 1:8). Apostleship was not so much the conferring of an honour on an outstanding servant of God as the laying of an obligation on him.

The apostles are here said to be *of Christ*. Apostleship is always conferred by a divine call, not by human commissioning (*cf.* Gal. 1:1). In Acts 1:24 the prayer before lots were cast on Joseph and Matthias ran, 'Show us which of these two you have chosen'. The apostle was already chosen by God, and the only thing remaining was for him to be made known. So, when it was revealed that Matthias was the man, we read of nothing like an ordination or commissioning; simply 'he was added to the eleven apostles' (v. 26).[2]

It accords with this that when Paul recalls that the preachers

---

[1] This functionary was made the basis for a theory of the Christian ministry which held that the apostles had the full authority of Christ and that in due course they passed it on to the bishops. It is now generally agreed, however, that far too much was claimed for this official, and that the *shaliach* tells us very little about the Christian apostle.

[2] See further my *Ministers of God* (Inter-Varsity Fellowship, 1964), ch. III.

were apostles he is thinking of responsibility rather than privilege; they had been set apart by God to preach the gospel. This did give them a place of honour and authority, but he insists that they had not claimed such a place, and indeed goes on to show that they had been more conscious of their responsibility than of their privileges.

Because the preachers were apostles they *could have been a burden* to the converts. The noun translated *a burden* (*baros*) is ambiguous; it may mean 'burden' or it may mean 'importance' (as LB, 'we certainly had a right to some honor'; NEB manages to get something of both meanings with 'we might have made our weight felt'). Paul may be saying that the apostles had the right to be treated with honour (though they had not sought it), or he may mean that they had the right to maintenance (and had not claimed it).

It is plain that Paul is repudiating any suggestion that the apostles had taken a high and mighty line and extracted money for their support from their converts. But his precise line of reasoning is not so clear. NIV reads *we were gentle*, and many, perhaps most, commentators would support this. But a large group of MSS reads 'we were (or became) babies among you'. There is a difference of one letter only in the Greek (*ēpioi* 'gentle' and *nēpioi* 'babies'), and this is the last letter of the preceding word. It could have been slipped in accidentally from that word, or it could have been omitted by a scribe who had already written one *n*. The difficulty is made more acute by the fact that, while 'gentle' seems to give the better sense, 'babies' has the better manuscript attestation. Those who favour 'gentle' point out that it is hard to think of Paul comparing himself to a baby and a nurse in the same sentence; that *nēpios* has the thought of being undeveloped and unripe and, when Paul uses it, it generally has some implication of blame; that *ēpios* occurs in the New Testament elsewhere only once (2 Tim. 2:24), and there is always a tendency for less usual forms to be assimilated to the more usual. In favour of 'babies' is the manuscript evidence;[1] the fact that Paul has no great objection to mixing his metaphors and indeed in this very chapter likens himself both

---

[1] It is accepted by the majority in Bruce M. Metzger, *A Textual Commentary on the Greek New Testament* (United Bible Societies, 1971), pp. 629–630.

to a father (v. 11) and to an orphan (v. 17, where 'torn away' is literally 'being orphaned'); after *apostles* a noun is more likely than an adjective; the Greek rendered *among you* is natural after 'babies', less so after 'gentle'; and what Westcott and Hort call 'the change from the bold image to the tame and facile adjective' which they think 'characteristic of the difference between St Paul and the Syrian revisers'.[1]

With the evidence so evenly balanced a firm decision is not possible, but I am inclined to go along with the weight of the mss and accept 'babies' as original. While it would be easy to alter the original either way, the probability of a change from 'babies' to 'gentle' seems greater than the reverse. If this be the reading the meaning would seem to be (with Origen and Augustine): 'like a nurse among her children talking in baby language'. It would indicate the tender way the preachers adapted themselves to their hearers. They took up no attitude of superiority.

The word that NIV renders as *mother* (as also GNB, JB, LB, *etc.*) really means 'nurse'; the reason for this translation is the statement that the children are her own. Paul's point is that a nurse would be expected to be *caring* with any children, but this would be especially the case with her own. The verb *caring* means basically 'to warm'; it is used of the mother bird (Dt. 22:6), and so comes to have the secondary meaning, 'to cherish', 'to care for tenderly'.

8. The apostles behaved in a genuinely affectionate manner towards the Thessalonians; Paul repeats the thought in different words: *we loved you so much*. He uses an unusual verb (*homeiromenoi*), and, while it cannot be proved, Wohlenberg's conjecture that it may be a term of endearment derived from the nursery (cited in Milligan) is very attractive, and may well be right. At any rate the verb does express a yearning over the converts, and a good will that is repeated in *we were delighted* (*eudokoumen*).

The preachers *were delighted* to impart *the gospel of God* to the Thessalonians; not only so, but they shared their *lives as well*.

[1] 'Notes on Select Readings', p. 128 (Appendix to Westcott and Hort, *The New Testament in the Original Greek*, Introduction (Macmillan, 1882)).

AV translates *psychas* as 'souls', while a number of translations join NIV with *lives* (GNB, JB, LB). But *psychē* does not mean quite 'soul' or even 'life'; in a context like this it stands for the whole personality, 'our own selves' (RSV). Paul is speaking of that giving of oneself (and not simply a message that one has heard somewhere) that is of the very essence of genuine Christian teaching and evangelism. As Best puts it, 'The true missionary is not someone specialized in the delivery of the message but someone whose whole being, completely committed to a message which demands all, is communicated to his hearers.' There is an intensity of expression which is a rebuke to that tepid service that keeps the innermost self to oneself and is always a cause of ineffectiveness. Vital Christian service is costly.

Part of the reason for Paul's giving of himself is seen in the concluding words of the verse, which really mean 'for you became beloved to us', where 'beloved' points to the self-giving quality of *agapē* (see on 1:3).

9. Paul calls on his readers to remember the *toil and hardship* that the preachers had endured. If there is a distinction between the two terms, *toil* (*kopos*) will point to the weariness involved in labour, while *mochthos* means, as the translation indicates, the *hardship*. The combination which, as Lightfoot, Neil and others point out, employs similar sounds (like 'toil and moil'), makes it clear that the work the preachers had done had been hard and fatiguing. They had not been play-acting or making a token gesture. The double function of evangelism and earning their living had meant hard work for them, and this the Thessalonians knew quite well. Paul does not say what kind of work they did, but the apostle was a tentmaker (Acts 18:3), which probably means a worker in leather. The reason for the constant work (*night and day*), Paul says, was *in order not to be a burden to anyone while we preached the gospel of God to you*. The verb *preached* (*ekēryxamen*) denotes the action of a herald, who, of course, said what was given him to say. His work was to pass on a message, not to produce some high-flown oration elaborately adorned with ear-tickling phraseology, nor even to give a simple message to meet the need as he saw it. The fact that this is a favourite way of referring to the activity of the Christian preacher in the New Testament puts stress on the divine nature of the message. The gospel preacher is not at liberty to substitute his view of the need of the moment for the God-given message of the cross. This is underlined by the reference to *the gospel of God*, an expression we have met in verses 2, 8 (and substantially in v. 4; apart from this it is found in the New Testament only in Mk. 1:14; Rom. 1:1; 15:16; 2 Cor. 11:7; 1 Pet. 4:17). This deep-seated certainty that he was entrusted with a message of divine, not human, origin gave a note of urgency and conviction to all that Paul did and said. The conviction that the gospel is *of God* is an important factor in fervent and effectual preaching, whether in the apostolic age or any other.

3. *The preachers' behaviour* (2:10–12)

10. Paul solemnly maintains that the Thessalonians can bear testimony on his behalf (*you* is emphatic; 'you of all people'), and, so certain is he that the preachers' behaviour had been above reproach, that he says that God is witness, too (*cf.* v. 5). He uses three adverbs (adjectives in NIV) to describe their conduct, *holy, righteous and blameless*, and the older commentators sometimes made sharp distinctions between them. They took the first to refer to their behaviour towards God, the second to that towards the Thessalonians and the third to that towards themselves. But this division seems artificial for, as R. C. Trench puts it, Scripture 'recognizes all righteousness as one, as growing out of a single root, and obedient to a single law'.[1] NIV's translation with adjectives rather than adverbs can be justified, for even in classical Greek adverbs are sometimes used in this way (BDF 434 (2)). The first term, *holy* (*hosiōs*), points to the character involved in being set apart for God, and the second, *righteous* (*dikaiōs*), to conformity to a norm; for biblical writers that norm is the law of God. The third, *blameless* (*amemptōs*), means without cause for reproach. The combination makes an impressive witness to Paul's certainty that no accusation could fairly be levelled at the conduct of the little band of evangelists. And the fact that he so confidently appeals to the Thessalonians as witnesses shows that he was right. They had been there at

---

[1] R. C. Trench, *Synonyms of the New Testament* (Macmillan, ⁸1876), p. 329.

the time and knew at first hand what had happened. Paul is appealing to people who knew what the truth was.

He calls the Christians *you who believed*. So central is faith to the Christian scheme of things that Christians are often called simply 'believers'. But here, in addition to this use, Paul is probably making a contrast with his Jewish opponents who stood out as non-believers. Those people violently rejected the message and the messengers, but Paul expresses his confidence in the believers.

11–12. From the way the preachers had lived and commended the message Paul turns to the manner and the content of the preaching. He reminds his readers (*you know*) of the tenderness with which the gospel had been preached to them as well as of the thoroughgoing nature of the demands that had been made on them. He himself had been like a father to them, the very opposite of the deceiver and go-getter he had been misrepresented as being. His loving care comes through in his insistence that he had brought the message to *each of you*, where the Greek 'each one' is more emphatic ('intensified', BDF 305) than the simple 'each'. In other words, he had not contented himself with giving the message in general terms to the Thessalonian public at large, but had been sufficiently interested in individuals to bring it home to them one by one, evidently in private conversations (*cf*. Phillips, 'how we dealt with each one of you personally').

Paul uses three verbs to convey the manner of the preaching, the combination giving the impression of urgency. The apostles had evidently been very much in earnest. The first verb carries the note of exhortation and encouragement. Being a Christian in first-century Thessalonica could not have been easy and the preachers had given the encouragement that was needed. The note of tenderness is intensified in the second verb, *comforting*, a verb used elsewhere in the New Testament only of comforting the faint-hearted (1 Thes. 5:14) or the bereaved (Jn. 11:19, 31). The preachers had been mindful of the difficulties that confronted the newly converted.

But, though there is this clear note of tenderness and understanding, it is also plain that the message was uncompromising.

The preachers had urged ('charged', rsv) the converts *to live lives worthy of God*, which sets before us 'the noblest possible ideal of life' (*CBSC*). Clearly Paul had not toned down the demands of the gospel in any way, and we are reminded that, when we become followers of Christ, no less a demand is made on us. More literally the expression means 'to walk worthily of God', where the metaphor of walking (as often in the New Testament) gives the idea of steady, if unspectacular, progress. There is nothing static about being a Christian.

God *calls you*, where the use of the present tense brings home the fact that God's call never ceases. Paul generally uses the past tense when he is referring to the call of God. He may use the aorist to remind us of the once-for-all nature of the call (*e.g.* Gal. 1:6, 15), or the perfect to point to the fact that those called remain in the position of called ones (*e.g.* 1 Cor. 7:15, 17). Here we see that God's call is always coming to us, and that it calls us to nothing less than being worthy of him. The Christian's standard is the highest possible.

God calls people *into his kingdom and glory*, the two concepts being closely linked (the Greek has a single preposition and article). The kingdom of God is the central topic of Jesus' teaching. It has Old Testament roots, for the idea that God rules over all is very ancient. But there was a new emphasis in Jesus' teaching and we appear to owe the very expression 'the kingdom of God' to him. Scholars are increasingly agreed that the concept is essentially dynamic; Jesus saw the kingdom as something that happens, as God's rule in action, rather than as something like a realm. In a sense the kingdom is present here and now, for God is working out his purposes and there are those who have yielded themselves to do his will. In another sense it is future, for not yet do we see all his enemies put under his feet (1 Cor. 15:24–25). The kingdom is closely associated with the person of Jesus, and, while the kingdom and the cross are not explicitly linked, we cannot but think that the death of the Christ was necessary to the establishment of the kingdom. It is a gift from God (Lk. 12:32), not the result of men's labours; it is not explicable but is always sheer miracle (Mk. 4:26–29). The thought of the Gospels is that God has broken into this world of space and time in the person of his

Son, and it is in this way that the kingdom is brought in.

The kingdom is not as central in the Pauline writings as in the Gospels, but Luke says that Paul could describe his ministry at Ephesus in the words, 'I have gone about preaching the kingdom' (Acts 20:25); at Rome 'he preached the kingdom of God' (Acts 28:31). There are some important references to it in the Epistles and a notable feature of Paul's understanding of the kingdom is that he speaks of it as Christ's, just as it is God's (Eph. 5:5; Col. 1:13). In the passage before us Paul has this great concept in mind.

4. *The preachers' message* (2:13)

Paul constantly gives thanks to God for the way the Thessalonians received the message the preachers brought. The expression translated *when you received the word of God* ('the word of divine preaching that goes out from us', BAGD) is difficult; more literally Paul refers to 'the word of hearing *(logon akoēs)*'. The word *akoē* means first the faculty of hearing (1 Cor. 12:17), then the organ of hearing, the ear (Mk. 7:35), then what is heard, the message. Paul is saying something like 'we handed on God's message' (NEB). Best points out that this noun is from the same root as *akouō*, 'to hear', and that among the Jews true hearing and obedience went together; here he sees the idea of 'obedient hearing'. Paul connects the hearing denoted by this noun with faith (Rom. 10:17; Gal. 3:2, 5), and the writer to the Hebrews looks for it to be accompanied by faith (Heb. 4:2). All this means that Paul appears to be thinking of the obedient response of faith that followed when the Thessalonians received the message. The verb *received (paralambanō)* is often used of the receiving of a tradition that has been handed on; Paul uses it of his own reception of the Christian message (1 Cor. 15:3). Neil sees it as a technical term for the reception of the *kērygma*, the message preached by Christian evangelists. The word *accepted (dechomai)* conveys the idea of a welcome, being the usual word for the reception of a guest (Ward calls it 'a hospitality word'). The message was not only heard and received by the Thessalonians; it was welcomed.

The reason for the welcome and for Paul's thanksgiving was that the Thessalonians received the message as truly *the word of*

God. Twice Paul insists that what the Thessalonians heard was *of God.* The second time is particularly emphatic, as we see from Findlay's rendering, 'you accepted no word of men, but, as it truly is, God's word' (*CGT*). Paul could preach with certainty and power, for he had the profound conviction that what he said was not of man's devising; it was the word of God, a conviction at the heart of the church's message. 'The man who feels that "there are few things worth living for and none worth dying for" will not gather around himself a band of zealous disciples' (Rolston). To preach interesting little moral essays can never prove an adequate substitute for the word that comes from God.

At the end of the verse Paul makes the point that this *word of God* really does things; it works in believers (*cf.* Rom. 1:16, where the gospel is said to be 'the power of God'). Most accept some such translation as NIV, *which is at work in you,* but Armitage Robinson, in a valuable note on *energein* (the verb here) and its cognates, argues that it should be understood as passive, *i.e.* 'is made operative'.[1] His point is that, while another writer may well have used the active, Paul prefers the passive which implies that God is the One who works. Whether we accept these linguistics or not, this is certainly Paul's thought; the power is God's and the word is his instrument (*cf.* NEB mg., 'God, who is at work'). The verb incidentally is almost always used in the New Testament with reference to supernatural activity (mostly that of God, though sometimes it refers to what Satan does).

5. Persecution (2:14–16)

14. *For* introduces the evidence for this working of God in the converts. That they had responded to the gospel as God's word is plain from the way they behaved. They became *imitators of God's churches in Judea.* This does not mean a conscious patterning of themselves on those churches, but rather that they had endured suffering in the same way. Paul has already linked their suffering with imitation (the imitation of the preachers and of their Lord, 1:6). It seems curious that he draws attention here

---

[1] Armitage Robinson, *St Paul's Epistle to the Ephesians* (Macmillan, 1904), pp. 241–247.

to the sufferings of the churches in Judea, when there were churches in the immediate neighbourhood that had suffered. We have no exact knowledge of the persecutions in Judea (though from Acts we can see the sort of thing that must have happened). But clearly they were well known throughout the Christian church and that may be the reason for referring to them. The early believers saw persecution as inevitable (*cf.* 2 Tim. 3:12).

15. Paul makes the point that the conduct of the Jews has been consistent; they have always been hostile to the purposes of God. When he says that they *killed the Lord Jesus*, by an unusual word order he manages to emphasize both *Lord* and *Jesus*. The One whom they killed was the Lord, with all that that means in terms of heavenly glory; and he was Jesus, fully man, and their fellow-countryman. In an important sense, of course, it was the Romans who actually killed Jesus, but Paul's point is that it was at the instigation of the Jews (*cf.* Jn. 18:30–31, 35; 19:10–15). Nor did this activity begin with Jesus, for they also killed *the prophets*; the New Testament writers often point to the way the Jews had treated the prophets (*cf.* Mt. 23:29–31, 35, 37; Lk. 11:47–51; 13:34; Acts 7:52; Rom. 11:3; *cf.* Mt. 5:12; Jas. 5:10). Nor did it finish there, for they *also drove us out* (the verb may also mean 'persecute severely', *cf.* AV, GNB). There is consistent opposition to God's way and God's people. Thus they *displease God* (they oppose his purposes) and *are hostile to all men* (they oppose the gospel which would bring blessing to all).

16. The indictment of the Jews continues. They have opposed the preaching of God's saving act among the Gentiles. Salvation is the comprehensive term, of which redemption, reconciliation and the like represent aspects. It is sometimes viewed as a salvation from evils like wrath (Rom. 5:9), or perdition (Phil. 1:28); sometimes it is a salvation with a view to blessings, such as the heavenly kingdom (2 Tim. 4:18). Here, as often, the term is used absolutely, with both positive and negative aspects implied.

The effect of the Jews' attitude on themselves includes their heaping up of *their sins to the limit*. Grammatically the words express the purpose of the Jews, but the sense of it is that God's purpose is worked out. Their continual hostility to his plan inevitably brings his wrath on them. They piled sin upon sin (Phillips, 'I fear they are completing the full tale of their sins'; *cf.* Mt. 23:32); the inevitable consequence is *the wrath of God* (as elsewhere, JB, NEB translate with 'retribution', but this is not what Paul says). The verb *has come* is in the aorist tense, which often denotes action in the past, but here the wrath is surely eschatological and therefore future. The aorist stresses the completeness and certainty of the coming of God's wrath. *At last* might be translated 'to the uttermost' (AV), and this seems to be Paul's meaning.

The denunciation of his own nation in these verses is unparalleled in Paul's writings and gives some indication of his feelings on the matter. As Neil says, he speaks like an Old Testament prophet, and his vigorous words leave no doubt as to the extent of the Jews' departure from the divine way. The castigation is unqualified, and the final expression indicating the eschatological wrath leaves no hope for the future. A nation (or a person) can reach a point in opposition to God where return is impossible.

IV. THE RELATIONSHIP OF PAUL TO THE THESSALONIANS (2:17 – 3:13)

A. PAUL'S DESIRE TO RETURN (2:17–18)

17. The adversative *But* puts Paul in contrast with the Jews, as does his use of the emphatic *we* (*hēmeis*). The apostle strongly desires to return to the scene of his labours, a desire arising from his deep regard for his converts. He calls them *brothers* and his word for *torn away* (*aporphanisthentes*) means literally 'having been orphaned'. The verb is used with some degree of freedom and is applied to other things than literal orphaning, but it is a strong word and fastens attention on Paul's sense of desolation. Already in this chapter he has compared himself to a mother (v. 7) and a father (v. 11); this is another example of his cheerful readiness to mix his metaphors if only he can make his point. His verb is used only here in the New Testament, but cognate words are used both metaphorically and literally (Jn. 14:18; Jas. 1:27); the use of the aorist may point to the sudden separation (Acts 17:10). The thought of being orphaned emphasizes his affection for those to whom he writes, as does the following *in person, not in thought*, where Phillips brings out the meaning with 'though never for a moment separated in heart' (LB 'our hearts never left you').

The longing is further expressed in the word translated *we made every effort*. The verb *spoudazō* combines the ideas of speed and diligence, and conveys an impression of eagerness, of making a quick and serious effort. In conjunction with this Paul uses the comparative adverb *perissoterōs*, 'exceedingly, more abundantly'. But, as the comparative has practically taken over the functions of the superlative in the New Testament, the meaning is probably 'very abundantly' or 'most abundantly' (though Milligan thinks that here the comparison is genuine; he paraphrases, 'we were exceedingly desirous to see you again face to face, and all the more so because of the hindrances we encountered'). The apostle's great eagerness to see his friends is further emphasized with the phrase *out of our intense longing*. The word *epithymia* means a strong passion, so that it is often translated 'lust' or 'covetousness'. This is one of the few places in the New Testament where it is used in a good sense.

18. *For* introduces the evidence for the longing just mentioned, namely that Paul eagerly *wanted to come*. The verb *wanted* (*thelō*) means 'willed'; clearly Paul is employing another word that will convey his strong desire to visit his friends. He slips in an exclamation that looks like a sudden outburst of personal feeling, being one of the few places in these two letters where the first person singular is used (see on 3:1), and the only place where the emphatic *egō* is found (*kagō* occurs in 3:5). The expression translated *again and again* (*kai hapax kai dis*) is unusual and appears to mean 'more than once' (so JB; see Introduction, p. 23); NIV is perhaps a little too strong. Paul is not speaking of a passing whim.

But he and his companions had been prevented from doing what they so much wanted to do. Just how *Satan stopped* them

Paul does not say; evidently the Thessalonians would recognize
the allusion. Modern suggestions are not convincing. Some
speak of illness, but it would be remarkable if this applied to all
three of them. Others think that Satan inspired the politarchs
to demand such surety as would keep the three away. But the
Thessalonians would know more about this than Paul, and it
would seem scarcely worth mentioning (there is also the difficulty of this happening 'more than once'). We should admit our
ignorance and understand the term in the most general sense.

Paul has no doubt about the activity of the evil spirit he calls
Satan. He is 'the tempter' (3:5), and probably 'the evil one'
(2 Thes. 3:3; see commentary, *ad loc.*). *Satan* is a Hebrew word
meaning 'accuser', 'adversary'; he is opposed to our best interests. Elsewhere Paul refers to 'the god of this age (or world)'
(2 Cor. 4:4) and to 'the ruler of the kingdom of the air' (Eph.
2:2). It is clear that Paul thought of Satan as having real existence; he is not using the term figuratively.

B. PAUL'S JOY (2:19–20)

19. At this point Paul is almost lyrical in his expressions of
esteem for his converts. *Our hope* shows his confidence in them,
and he also calls them *our joy* and *the crown in which we will
glory*. He comes back to glory and joy in the next verse; he
cannot find words too strong for what he has to say.

The crown of which he speaks (*stephanos*) is the laurel wreath
given to the victor at the games, or the festive garland, rather
than the *diadēma*, the royal diadem (though the distinction must
not be pressed, for *stephanos* is sometimes used of a royal
crown). *In which we will glory* renders *kauchēseōs*, sometimes
translated 'boasting'; it means that the joy was expressed outwardly as well as felt inwardly.

We should probably take the question *Is it not you?* as a
parenthesis, to give the meaning 'What is our hope . . . (is it
not you?) in the presence . . .'. We should also notice an ambiguity. There is a *kai* (='even' or 'too') before *you*; Paul may be
asking whether his joy, *etc.*, is not the very people he is accused
of abandoning ('even you', 'you of all people'), or he may mean

'you as well as others – you are no special case'. Notice further that Paul combines the title *Lord* (the one who is in the highest place) with the human name *Jesus* (*Christ* is not in the older MSS and should be omitted). 'Lord Jesus' or 'Lord Jesus Christ' occurs twenty-four times in the eight chapters of these two letters, which is more often than anywhere else in the New Testament. Acts, for example, has it seventeen times and Romans sixteen. This frequent use of 'Lord' may well be because in these two letters the second coming is so much in mind. This is certainly the case here, for Paul goes on to refer to it immediately (*when he comes*). This is the first occurrence of *parousia* in Christian literature. It means basically 'presence' (as in 2 Cor. 10:10, where NIV has 'in person'), but it came to be used as a technical expression for a royal visit.[1] In the New Testament it became the accepted term for the second coming of the Lord, and this is a typical example of its use.

20. There is emphasis on both *you* and *are*. The Thessalonians (and no other) are (not will be) Paul's cause for pride and joy. Of the two words he uses, *glory* refers to their giving him cause for honouring them before other people and *joy* to his own feelings of delight. Outwardly and inwardly the Thessalonian converts crowned his ministry.

C. TIMOTHY'S MISSION (3:1–5)

This passage, with its obvious and deep concern for the spiritual well-being of the converts, is a revealing glimpse of Paul's pastoral concern ('the very essence of the spirit of the pastor', Barclay).

1. The chapter division here is unfortunate. *So* links what follows to what has preceded. It is because of the things just mentioned that Timothy's mission was undertaken.

To whom does *we* refer? The first person plural is a problem not only here, but throughout the Epistle. On the one hand,

[1] See Deissmann, *LAE*, pp. 358–373.

Silvanus and Timothy are associated with Paul in the opening salutation; on the other, the style seems just as Pauline as in any letter accepted as coming from the great apostle's hand, and some of the things said seem to refer to Paul alone. The difficulty is especially great here. The singular is rare in these letters (1 Thes. 2:18; 3:5; 5:27; 2 Thes. 2:5; 3:17), from which it is possible to infer either that in most places Paul uses the epistolary plural (meaning 'I') but has an occasional lapse into the singular, or that his plural is genuine, meaning all three, and that his 'I' is a personal comment added in a few places. There is an emphatic use of the singular in verse 5, which some take to mean the same as the plural here, while others see it as in contrast, which would mean that this is a genuine plural. There is an immediate difficulty in the way of a genuine plural; it is hard to see Timothy as sending himself (v. 2). This leads to the suggestion that Paul and Silvanus are meant (Ward, Hendriksen). I cannot think this an attractive solution. A plural applying to all three authors is understandable, as is an epistolary plural that means Paul only. But a plural meaning two out of three is far from easy. Moreover 'alone' at the end of the verse is also plural (*monoi*; NIV *by ourselves*), though it seems to refer to Paul alone, and the natural assumption is that the verb also refers to him alone. It seems best to take the *we* as epistolary, though we need not think that Paul took the decision without consulting his helpers.

He speaks of his anxiety becoming intolerable. His verb, *stegō*, basically means 'to cover', then 'to hide by covering', 'to conceal', a meaning some accept here. But it also means 'to ward off by covering' and thus 'to bear up against', 'to endure', which gives the better sense in this passage (it is also the meaning in 1 Cor. 9:12; 13:7, its only New Testament occurrences outside this chapter).

Paul uses a strong term, *kataleipō*, to describe his being left in Athens; it can be used of abandoning (as in Eph. 5:31 of a man leaving his parents when he marries), and often of dying (*e.g.* Mk. 12:19). It expresses a sense of desolation, reinforced by the emphatic 'alone'. It was with a very real sense of deprivation that Paul had said goodbye to Timothy. Though he knew that his helper's departure had been necessary, he had felt

himself abandoned. He had had to face the cultured philo-
sophers and idolaters of Athens – and to face them alone.

2. Something of Paul's regard for Timothy comes out in
his unusually elaborate reference to him (he is generally 'our
brother'). We see, too, something of his high regard and deep
concern for his friends in Thessalonica, in that he was ready to
part with such a beloved friend and valued colleague at such a
time. A complicated textual problem makes it difficult to be
certain of the exact terms Paul uses. *Timothy . . . our brother* is
certain, but some MSS add 'and minister of God', some 'fellow-
labourer of God', some 'fellow-labourer', and there are other
readings. Our choice seems to be between 'minister of God'
(with better MSS attestation) and 'fellow-labourer of God', a startling expression (despite its occurrence in 1 Cor. 3:9), which
scribes would be more likely to alter to 'minister' than *vice versa*.
On the whole, it seems slightly more probable that 'minister'
(*diakonos*) is original, but we cannot be sure. This word was
used of the service of a table waiter, then of service in general,
and so of the specifically Christian service of God and man,
the sense in which it is used here. (It came to mean a 'deacon',
but that cannot be its meaning here.) Timothy is a minister 'in
the gospel of Christ' (the Greek does not say *spreading*; it is
serving the gospel, however that is done). Notice that it is
Christ's gospel; it is also called God's (2:2, 8, 9), that of our
Lord Jesus (2 Thes. 1:8), and 'ours' (1:5; 2 Thes. 2:14).

The purpose of sending Timothy was *to strengthen and encourage you in your faith*. The verb *strengthen* seems to have been
a technical term in the early church (so Best; Swete on Rev. 3:2).
It occurs often in the New Testament and brings home to us
that it is not sufficient to have had a spectacular conversion. We
must go on and be established and strengthened in the faith.
The verb translated *encourage* is akin to the noun 'Counsellor',
used of the Holy Spirit (Jn. 14:16, 26, *etc.*); it emphasizes the
ideas of strengthening and helping. The preposition *hyper* (*in*)
probably retains something of its original force of 'for the ad-
vantage or benefit of' (so Milligan).

3. There is some difficulty about the meaning of *sainesthai*,

translated *unsettled*. Many take it as NIV, but Homer and others use the verb of a dog wagging its tail, whence it comes to signify 'to fawn upon', 'to flatter'. If we accept this meaning (and the usage of the word seems to indicate that we should), then Paul is saying that Timothy's mission was in order that the converts should not be cajoled with smooth talk when they were in the midst of persecution. It is likely that, while the Gentiles were persecuting them, the Jews were urging them to abandon the Christian way and accept Judaism, which would, of course, immediately free them from their plight. This is supported by Paul's use of *en*, 'in these trials'; the word can mean *by* (as NIV), but it seems that the apostle is referring to the smooth talk of the Jews 'in' the trials rather than to the trials themselves.

The concluding part of verse 3 is a sobering reminder that afflictions are not to be taken as something strange and unusual for the believer: *we were destined for them*. Paul links himself with the Thessalonians with his use of *we* and he uses an expressive verb (*keimai*, practically the perfect of *tithēmi*), used for example of 'a city set on a hill' (Mt. 5:14), and of Paul as being 'put here' for the defence of the gospel (Phil. 1:16). There is a sense of immovability about it, of unchangeable divine appointment. Affliction, then, is no accident, but an integral part of the life of the Christian (*cf.* Jn. 16:33; Acts 14:22).

4. Paul's certainty about the reality of tribulation was not a new discovery, but had already had its place in his first preaching to the Thessalonians. We should probably regard the use of the imperfect tense (*proelegomen*) as significant, and translate 'we repeatedly foretold' (NIV *we kept telling you*), which harmonizes with his repeated statement that the converts knew these things. There is another hint at the certainty and divine ordination of tribulation in the verb rendered *would* (*mellomen*, not the simple future; there is a similar note of divine assurance in Rom. 8:13, 18, *etc.*). Paul had not only made a prediction; he had seen his words fulfilled, as the Thessalonians could testify.

5. Paul repeats the thought of verse 1, though with a greater emphasis on his personal feeling and activity; he takes the unusual course in this letter of using the first person singular

(*kagō* only here; *egō* in 2:18). Those who hold that *we* in verse 1 includes Paul's friends take this to mean, in contrast, Paul's personal action. But if we regard that 'we' as an epistolary plural, this repeats and gives emphasis to what Paul has already said.

T. W. Manson understands *pistin* here as 'faithfulness' rather than *faith*,[1] but it would seem on inadequate grounds. The word can have that meaning, and it would not be inappropriate here. But in the New Testament its more usual meaning is 'faith', and, as it seems to have that meaning in verse 2, it is better to take it in the same sense here. Paul had sent to make inquiry about their faith, *i.e.* whether it had survived the time of testing, whether it included the grace of perseverance. The Greek does not read *I was afraid*; the word is *mē* and we should translate it in some such way as 'lest'.

There is an interesting change of construction. Paul uses the indicative when he says, *the tempter might have tempted you*, which leaves the impression that he thinks this has probably happened. But his change to the subjunctive in *our efforts might have been useless* makes this proposition open to doubt. Paul thinks it probable that Satan has applied pressure to his converts, but improbable that they have given way. *The tempter*, of course, is Satan (see comment on 2:18). The word translated *efforts* (*kopos*) means wearisome toil. His ministry at Thessalonica had been no perfunctory one.

D. TIMOTHY'S REPORT (3:6–8)

6. *But . . . just now* introduces a new section, marking a break in the Greek. It shows that Paul was writing not long after Timothy had made his report. Moffatt renders 'a moment ago', which is a trifle too strong, but clearly Timothy's arrival was very recent.

Timothy *brought good news*, where the verb (*euangelizomai*) is that generally used for 'preach the gospel'; it shows how remarkably Paul had been affected by Timothy's news. This seems

[1] *BJRL*, 35, 1952–53, p. 440, n. 2.

to be the only place in the New Testament where the word is used of any other news than God's saving work (Rev. 10:7 may be an exception; Heb. 4:2, 6 include that work in Old Testament times). Masson reminds us that Paul never speaks of faith without thinking of Christ; thus the good news of the faith and love of the converts is not unlike the good news of Christ (v. 2). The news was a veritable gospel for Paul, reminding him of the faithfulness and the power of God. It put new heart into him and enabled him to go about his work with vigour and certainty. The Thessalonians had shown *faith and love*; they had not been wanting in the right attitude either to God or to man.

But the good news did not stop there. Not only were the converts sound in doctrine and impeccable in conduct; they also retained warm feelings towards Paul. They had *pleasant memories* of the preachers and longed to see them again, where the verb *epipotheō* marks an intensity of feeling (as it nearly always does; *cf.* 2 Cor. 5:2; Phil. 1:8; 2:26). The yearning for a reunion was mutual and reveals once more something of Paul's tender regard for his Thessalonian converts.

7. The address *brothers* expresses affection, and Paul goes on to speak of being encouraged (*cf.* v. 2) on the basis of (*epi*) the *faith* of his friends. The same preposition (*epi*) is used with *all our distress and persecution*. But this time the meaning is closer to the word's literal sense 'over', and hints at rising 'above' the difficulties. These are serious troubles, *distress* (*anankē*) being basically 'the choking, pressing care', and *persecution* (*thlipsis*) 'the crushing trouble' (Lightfoot). They combine to emphasize that Paul's situation was far from a happy one when the encouragement he speaks of reached him (see Introduction, p. 20).

8. This leads to the thought that it is life to him to know that his converts are standing fast. *Now* is probably temporal, 'at the present time', though the logical sense 'this being so' is not impossible (and in this case perhaps not so very different). Paul uses the present tense in the verb *live*; it was not a passing burst of inspiration he got from the news from Thessalonica, but something that remained, and would remain with him. This

is more than physical life; it is all the fullness of the Christian life. Translations like 'now we can breathe again' (JB; cf. NEB) seem to miss this.

Paul uses the emphatic pronoun *you*, which may indicate that he attached special importance to the Thessalonians' endurance. In a sense they were a test case, and the successful propagation of the gospel in other places depended on their standing firm as a living testimony to the power of God. Certainly Paul is stressing that for him a lot depended on them. His verb for *standing* (*stēkō*) is not the usual one, but a late form which has something of the idea of firmness about it (standing *firm*). The construction in the conditional clause is unusual; *ean* usually takes the subjunctive, but here has the indicative, which adds a touch of definiteness. Findlay says that it 'states the hypothesis more assertively', and the clause 'is a virtual appeal; "You must show that my misgiving was needless; you will go on to justify my confidence" ' (*CGT*). The conviction that 'you will go on' is noteworthy. It is important that the standing is *in the Lord*. They have a right relationship to Christ and are not standing in their own strength.

E. PAUL'S SATISFACTION (3:9–10)

This leads to an expression of Paul's pleasure at the turn of events in Thessalonica; first he asks a rhetorical question, and then prays that he might be able to come and see his friends.

9. *How can we thank God enough for you?* he asks. By human standards what has happened was a tribute to the work Paul had done and was something of a personal triumph (so Neil). The church had been so well established that, though the believers were young in the faith and had been subjected to such stern tests, they had come through with flying colours, and their founder might well feel proud of his work. But Paul realized that what had happened was due to the divine power in the believers, and thus he gives thanks to God for his goodness in this matter. AV translates more literally 'what thanks can we render . . . ?' (so NASB), where the verb 'render' (*antapodidōmi*) carries the notion of something due (*cf.* 2 Thes. 1:6; Lk. 14:14, *etc.*). There is probably a similar recognition of what is due in that Paul's joy is *in the presence of our God*, where he deepens his joy by 'referring it to its true author' (Milligan).

10. Paul's fervent longing to see the Thessalonians again finds expression in constant and fervent prayer. Praying *night and day* is emphatic enough, but he adds an expressive and unusual adverb (*hyperekperissou*; elsewhere in the New Testament only in 5:13; Eph. 3:20). It is a double compound, giving a twofold addition to the original 'abundantly'; one gets the impression of a man struggling to put into words a feeling too deep for words. Of the verbs meaning 'pray' he chooses *deomai*, which expresses need or lack (rather than *proseuchomai*, with its stress on devotion to God). Combined with the adverb it draws attention to Paul's sense of loss in his separation from his friends and thus to his regard for them.

There are two points in his continual prayer: the first that Paul may be reunited with the Thessalonians, the second that he may *supply what is lacking in* their *faith*. The verb *katartizō* means 'to make complete', and it is used of such an activity as mending nets (Mt. 4:21), though in the New Testament it is more often metaphorical. It is translated 'restore' (Gal. 6:1), where the thought is that of correction, not punishment. The meaning may be equipping (Heb. 10:5, 'prepared'; 11:3, 'formed'), or, as here, of supplying what is missing for the full discharge of the functions for which a thing or person is designed.

What is lacking translates the noun *hysterēma*, 'deficiency', 'shortcoming'. In spite of his great enthusiasm for the spiritual achievement of these converts, Paul recognizes that they come short of what they should be. Even here, when he is giving full rein to his desire to see them and his joy in their stand, he yet finds a prominent place for this pastoral work of building them up wherever their faith is defective. It is a mark of Paul's tact that he speaks first of the things wherein he can sincerely praise them, and only then indicates that there are other things to be taken into consideration. Calvin found in this verse an indication of the importance of Christian teaching: 'From this also it appears how necessary it is for us to give careful attention to doctrine, for teachers were not appointed merely with the view of leading men, in the course of a single day or month, to the faith of Christ, but for the purpose of perfecting the faith which has been begun.'

F. PAUL'S PRAYER (3:11–13)

From a rhetorical question Paul now turns to an actual prayer (not many agree with Hendriksen that this is not a prayer but 'the devout utterance of a wish'). His petition is twofold, first that he might be brought to Thessalonica, and secondly that the Christians there might increase in love.

11. Some have seen in the opening words, *Now may our God and Father himself*, an emphatic contrast, either with human activity (*i.e.* prayer, v. 10), or with Satan (undersood; *cf.* 2:18). But this seems unnecessary; we simply have the introduction of a new section, together with what Lightfoot calls 'an outburst of the earnest conviction which was uppermost in the Apostle's mind of the utter worthlessness of all human efforts without the divine aid'.

Notice that *our God and Father* is linked in the closest fashion in the address of this prayer with *our Lord Jesus* (again in 2 Thes. 2:16, in the reverse order), and that the verb (*kateuthynai*) is in the singular. There could scarcely be a more impressive way of indicating the lordship of Christ, and his oneness with the Father (*cf. EGT*, the singular 'implies that God and Jesus count as one in this connection'). From a very early time (this letter is dated about AD 50) Christians accepted the deity of our Lord without question. (Prayer is not the place for the introduction of argument.) Prayer is offered to God alone; only one who was divine could be bracketed in this way with the Father. The prayer is that God and Christ may *clear the way, i.e.* remove the obstacles that Satan has put in the path.

12. The second part of the prayer is introduced with an emphatic 'But you' (*hymas de*). Whatever the Lord may have in store for Paul and his companions, he prays that spiritual blessing may abound for his readers. By *the Lord* he almost certainly means Jesus, but as we see from the preceding petition he is making no great distinction between the Father and the Son. For him both were God and the two were in some sense one. His prayer is for spiritual enlargement for his friends, and more particularly for enlargement in love, a quality in which they were not lacking (1:3; 4:9–10). The two verbs, *increase* and *overflow*, are more or less synonymous and together constitute a petition for the most abundant blessing. Some understand *increase* to refer to numerical increase, but this is not the meaning. Rather the two verbs are to be taken together and the following 'in love' goes with both (RSV 'make you increase and abound in love').

It is characteristic of the Christian outlook that the prayer is for love *for each other and for everyone else*. Neil comments that, while love for each other was 'no more than the Gentiles practised', love for all men was more difficult and 'could only come as a gift from God'. But the specifically Christian quality denoted by *agapē* is never natural to man; it comes only to those who have been transformed by the power of God. Whether it is exercised towards believers or non-believers, *agapē* is the gift of God. This, indeed, is implied in the fact that Paul makes it a matter for prayer. He speaks first of love within the brotherhood and then of that for outsiders (*cf.* Best, 'It is easier to love those who love us and loving within the Christian community may then be a school for learning to love those outside'; *cf.* Gal. 6:10, and for a similar thought about peace, Rom. 12:17–18). Paul is, of course, well aware that, if he would teach others, he must first teach himself. As he does elsewhere in these Epistles, he appeals to the example he and his companions had set; their love for the Thessalonians was plain.

13. The purpose of this abounding love is now given. The verb *strengthen* is used in verse 2 (where see note). In LXX it is also combined with 'heart' (Ps. 104:15; 112:8). *Hearts*, as in 2:4, does not refer simply to the emotional side of human nature (as with us), but is the comprehensive term for the whole of our inner states, thoughts, feelings and will. It stands for the

77

whole personality. Paul is saying that our whole personality is established on a firm foundation only when there is a basis of abundant love. The self-centred person at best will have an element of weakness and instability. But where anyone has learned to love the Lord his God with all his heart, and his neighbour as himself, then he has a firm foundation for life.

Paul prays that God will 'establish your hearts unblamable in holiness' (RSV, where 'holiness' is the state of sanctity rather than the process of becoming holy). In LXX this word is used only of God; it is the very highest degree of holiness that Paul wants for his friends. It is holiness *in the presence of our God*; a person may have high moral standards, even humanly speaking to the extent of being blameless, and yet not be holy. This had been Paul's state in his pre-Christian years (Phil. 3:6, where 'faultless' is the word he uses here). Holiness has an essential God-ward reference; it denotes the quality of being set apart for God, and the Christian should display it in pre-eminent measure.

Paul reinforces this with a reminder of the second coming of the Lord *with all his holy ones*. Who are these *holy ones*? The word 'holiness' in the Bible means being set apart for God, and, as that is a characteristic of all who believe, the usual New Testament name for believers is simply 'holy ones' or 'saints'. 'Saints' are not people who have won the special approbation of the church because of their outstanding goodness; they are ordinary church members. But it does not seem likely that the term here means ordinary church members, for it is to ordinary church members that the words are addressed and the 'holy ones' in question will be coming to them at the parousia.

Two suggestions are offered. 'Holy ones' may be angels (so, for example, Masson; *cf.* Mk. 8:38), or they may be the saints who have departed this life (*cf.* JB, RSV, *etc.*). In favour of the first suggestion is the fact that angels seem sometimes to be meant by the expression 'the holy ones' in the Old Testament (Ps. 89:5; Dn. 4:13 (Th.); 8:13; Zc. 14:5). Further, angels are more than once associated with the Lord at his coming again (Mt. 13:41; 25:31; Mk. 8:38; Lk. 9:26; 2 Thes. 1:7). On the other hand, angels seem never to be referred to simply as 'the holy ones' in the New Testament. There the term almost invariably refers to people (albeit people here on earth, 'the saints').

But it seems clear that there will be believers associated with Christ at the parousia (4:14; *cf.* their part in judging, 1 Cor. 6:2). Most favour the view that 'the saints' are in mind (though without a convincing explanation of why the Thessalonians are not included). But the term is comprehensive and it may be better to see it as including all who will be with the Lord when he returns; *all* seems difficult to restrict to one group (*cf.* Neil, Milligan, *etc.*).

V. EXHORTATION TO CHRISTIAN LIVING (4:1–12)

As is usual in the Pauline writings, after some solid doctrine we have a concluding section (introduced by *oun*, 'therefore') drawing out the application of the teaching to Christian living. Because the doctrine is true, consequences follow for the way we live.

A. GENERAL (4:1–2)

1. There are divergent views about the Greek translated *finally* (*loipon oun*). While C. F. D. Moule accepts this rendering,[1] Whiteley forthrightly refers to it as a 'mistranslation', and Bailey argues that it simply marks a transition. Paul can use it quite early in a letter (1 Cor. 1:16), but as used here it seems to mean that the main argument has been concluded, though other, not unimportant, matters are now to be dealt with.

Paul uses the affectionate address, *brothers*, and reminds his readers that they had already been told how they should live out their Christian faith (*live* is actually 'walk'; the Christian way means steady if unspectacular progress). *How to live* is really 'how you must live'; pleasing God is not a matter of personal choice, but an imperative necessity for the Christian. *We instructed you* is rather 'you received' (*paralambanō*; see on

[1] Moule, *IBNTG*, p. 161.

2:13) 'from us'; they received the authentic Christian tradition. Now, Paul says, *we ask you and urge you*, where there is not much difference between his two verbs (Best regards them as synonymous, but Thomas differentiates them); perhaps the first signifies 'request' and the second 'urge'. *In the Lord Jesus* is basic to the whole exhortation. Paul does not presume to urge a line of conduct on them because of his personal stature or knowledge, but because this is the kind of conduct that should characterize those who are in Christ, as he is and they are.

The purpose is that the Thessalonians should *do this more and more*, where the verb means 'abound' as in 3:12 ('overflow'); there it is used of abounding in love, but here it is used absolutely, a use that brings out the thought that the Christian life is the more abundant life (*cf.* Jn. 10:10). It is the only life that really frees people.

2. The word for *instructions* (*parangelias*) is not common in Christian writings, being found elsewhere in the New Testament with reference to commands in the faith twice only (1 Tim. 1:5, 18; the cognate verb occurs more often). Properly it signifies an order passed from one to another, as when a command is passed along a line of soldiers, and it is often used for military orders. It is thus very appropriate for authoritative commands, such as those given *by the authority of the Lord Jesus*. The preposition *by* is *dia*, which makes it clear that the commands were not Paul's but God's (they came 'through' Jesus). There does not seem much difference from 'in the Lord Jesus' (v. 1), but 'in' may perhaps be more dynamic. But the repetition of the idea makes it clear that Paul is not concerned with merely human directions. He had from the beginning shown them the way of God, and this is what he continues to do.

B. SEXUAL PURITY (4:3–8)

A marked feature of life in the first-century Roman Empire, and specifically in Greece, was sexual laxity. The Thessalonian Christians lived in a world where people did not see fornication as a sin, but as part of normal life. It featured in the worship of more than one deity, and men in general found it difficult to feel deeply on the subject. But in this, as in many things, the Christians refused to take their standards from contemporary society. They insisted that sexual vice incurs the wrath of God and that it is to be avoided scrupulously by every follower of Christ. This makes Paul's words very relevant to our age, an age not conspicuous for high moral standards. As Neil trenchantly puts it, 'In our own semi-pagan society it needs to be stated again as firmly as Paul does here. "Affairs" are not a source of easy laughs for radio or variety comedians, but – more properly described as promiscuous fornication – are one of the Seven Deadly Sins.'

3. Paul puts the subject on the highest plane with his opening, *It is God's will* (NIV omits his 'for', which ties this into the preceding argument). In the Greek *will* has no article, signifying that what follows is not the whole will of God. There are many things included in God's will, but one is certainly the injunction that follows. Christians must not concern themselves only with those things that appeal to them. They must have regard to the fact that God is interested in all that they do, and God's will is that they should be pure. 'Your sanctification' (NASB) points to the process of which 'holiness' is the completed state. From the moment anyone believes, he is set apart for God, set apart to be 'holy'; in New Testament language he is a 'saint'. As we saw in the comment on 3:13, this does not mean that he is morally perfect, but that he is given over to God to do his will. Thus a process is begun in which the old ways and the old habits are increasingly done away and replaced with new ways that fit the service of God. This is a long and necessary process, and much of the New Testament is taken up with instruction as to how it may be furthered. Here Paul lays it down firmly that it is God's will that God's people live in God's way.

The particular aspect of sanctification in mind is sexual purity. Negatively this means *that you should avoid sexual immorality.* Paul's word is *porneia*, which strictly means 'fornication', but is used in New Testament times for any kind of sexual sin. The Christian is to have nothing to do with it (*cf.* Phillips, 'and that entails first of all a clean cut with sexual immorality').

4. Positively, each should keep himself in sanctification and honour. It is interesting that Paul uses the verb 'know' (NIV *learn*); it is as though this sin is unthinkable in anyone who knows what the Christian faith implies. This is capable of wider application, for the Christian faith reaches into all of life and uplifts all it touches. Paul repeats his word 'sanctification' from verse 3, for this mastery of self is to be looked for in those who walk the way of holiness. With this he links 'honour', for sexual impurity brings dishonour and shame.

There is a problem about the meaning of the word translated *body* (*skeuos*). The word literally means 'vessel', which many of the early Greek commentators took to mean 'body', though *skeuos* does not seem to have this meaning elsewhere. But in Greek writers generally the body is sometimes thought of as the instrument or container of the soul, and, while this is not a New Testament thought, there are passages that contrast the real 'I' with the body (*e.g.* 2 Cor. 4:7; 5:1–4, 6–8), and some where 'vessel' means people (Acts 9:15; Rom. 9:22–23; 2 Tim. 2:21). But Theodore of Mopsuestia, Augustine and others took the word to mean 'wife'[1] here and many accept this view today. It is supported by the fact that the verb translated 'to control', which more literally means 'to acquire', is not very suitable for 'body' but is found in LXX and elsewhere of marrying a wife. Support is also sought in the reference to the wife as 'the weaker vessel' (1 Pet. 3:7, AV). This last point does not count for much, for (a) both husband and wife are 'vessels' in this verse, the wife being the 'weaker', and (b) both are vessels of the Holy Spirit. The wife is not the husband's 'vessel'.

The big difficulty in the way of 'body' is the verb 'acquire'. But there is evidence that it can mean what follows from acquiring, *i.e.* 'possess' (MM cite a papyrus dated AD 23 where a man declares an oath that he 'has' thirty days to produce a man he bailed out of jail; they think that here the meaning is 'gradually obtain the complete mastery of the body'); the difficulty is not insuperable. Against 'wife' are two strong arguments. One

---

[1] Ch. Maurer finds *kᵉlî*, the Hebrew equivalent of *skeuos*, used in Rabbinic writings of the woman 'only in a figurative sense'. But 'to use as a vessel' *etc.* 'are established euphemisms for sexual intercourse' (*TDNT*, vii, p. 362). J. Whitton argues for the meaning 'body' in the sense 'mastering one's sexual urge' (*NTS*, 28, 1982, pp. 142–143).

is that it demands a low view of marriage (*i.e.* that the primary function of the wife is to satisfy her husband's sexual desires) just where Paul is advocating a high view. The other is that there is no reason for holding that the words apply only to the male section of the church. The letter is written to the whole church (masculine forms like *his* arise because the Greek masculine embraces both sexes in such contexts). Neither single nor married ladies could acquire a wife, but all, of both sexes, married and single, should control their bodies. Our best understanding is that Paul is calling on the Thessalonians to keep their bodies pure (perhaps in the style of 1 Cor. 6:18–20).

5. They are to do this 'not in the passion of lust' (RSV). The former of these two nouns, *pathos*, properly denotes 'a feeling which the mind suffers' (GT), and so a passion. It 'signifies not, like Eng. "passion," a violent feeling, but an overmastering feeling, in which the man is borne along by evil as though its passive instrument' (Findlay, *CGT*). It is the passive side of a vice, whereas the following *epithymia*, 'lust', is the active side. The combination points to the surrender to one's passions.

This surrender was common in the world of that day, and Paul goes on to say that it was characteristic of *the heathen* (*ta ethnē*), a term often translated 'the Gentiles'. It usually denotes non-Jewish nations, but sometimes, as here, people outside the Christian church. Their characteristic is that they *do not know God*. This does not mean that God had given them no revelation of himself, but that they had rejected the light they had (*cf.* Rom. 1:18–32). Paul speaks not of an innocent ignorance, but of blameworthy neglect of the light they had received, so that they were given up to unnatural lusts (Rom. 1:19–20, 24–27). Unbelief often has its basis in the rejection of the light God has given.

6. The Greek rendered *in this matter* is literally 'in the matter' and some think there is a change of subject, with business affairs now in mind. But NIV is surely right in seeing 'the' matter as the one just mentioned. While the verbs used could be meaningful if applied to business affairs, they are also significant when sex is in mind. Sexual sin, besides being an offence against holiness and honour, is an act of fraud against a *brother*; it takes what is rightly his. In this sense *brother*, of course, means 'brother man', not 'brother in Christ'. What Paul says applies obviously to adultery; this wrongs others than the two parties. The same applies to pre-marital promiscuity; the impure person cannot bring to the marriage that virginity that is the other's due.

Such conduct cannot go unpunished. *The Lord will punish* (or, 'is an avenger', *cf.* Ps. 94:1), which means that he will do justice (*cf.* Rom. 13:4). God will punish *all such sins, i.e.* sins of uncleanness. This probably looks forward to the Day of Judgment, though there is a sense in which God's judgment operates in the here and now (Rom. 1:24, 26, 28). This was also part of Paul's preaching at Thessalonica; the preachers had *warned* of this (the verb means 'solemnly testified').

7. *For* ties this in to the argument (and probably refers back to vv. 3ff., not simply to the end of v. 6). The Christian life rests on the basis of God's call, not on human initiative. The idea of this call means a lot to Paul, though it is not frequent in the Thessalonian Epistles (see, however, 2:12; 5:24; 2 Thes. 2:14). From the time of his own spectacular conversion Paul was in no doubt that the primary fact is that God calls people, not that people decide to be God's. It is interesting to see this major Pauline concept so early.

There is a change of preposition: God did not call us 'for' uncleanness, where *epi* gives the idea of purpose (as in being called 'for freedom', Gal. 5:13, or of being created 'for good works', Eph. 2:10). *But to live a holy life* is rather 'in' holiness or sanctification; this is the atmosphere in which believers find themselves.[1] The noun is that referring to the process (as in v. 3) not the state (as in 3:13).

8. *Therefore* points us to a consequence. Because God has called us in sanctification it follows that those who treat this

---

[1] Nigel Turner sees as 'bluntly insensitive' the failure to make the distinction between *epi* and *en*. He translates: 'God has not called us *to* uncleanness, but his call is addressed to us *in our state of sanctification*' (*Grammatical Insights into the New Testament* (T. & T. Clark, 1965), p. 121).

lightly are despising no less a person than God himself. There is a little difficulty about the word *atheteō, rejects*; it is translated in various ways, *e.g.* 'set aside' (Gal. 2:21), 'frustrate' (1 Cor. 1:19). It means something like 'to treat as null and void', 'to regard as of no account', and that is its meaning here. The person who takes sexual sin lightly, who sees it as something that does not matter much, is, in effect, treating God as of no account, for the prohibition is his (*cf.* Lk. 10:16 for a similar thought).

The particular aspect of the divine activity singled out is his giving of the Holy Spirit, a continuing and present activity. It is not that the offenders despise a God who gave the Spirit a long time ago, but one who keeps on giving him. Their sin is a sin against the continuing presence of the Spirit (*cf.* 1 Cor. 6:19).

In an unusual word order Paul speaks of 'the Spirit of him the holy', a more stately expression than that usually employed and one which emphasizes both the majesty of the Spirit and the holiness that is such a feature of this passage. He also says that the Spirit is given to *you*. He might have left the statement general, but he makes it personal to the Thessalonians.

C. BROTHERLY LOVE (4:9–10)

9. Two things in particular marked off the Christians of New Testament days from contemporary society: the purity of their lives and the love that they practised so fully. Here Paul passes from the one to the other. *Brotherly love* (*philadelphia*) is not the same as *agapē*, the love towards all that must characterize those who have experienced the *agapē* of God (see on 1:3).[1] It is to be exercised by the Christian towards all people, irrespective of their merit or the reverse. But he should also exercise a special *brotherly love* to those united with him in the household of faith. Outside the New Testament *philadelphia* almost invariably denotes the love that binds together the children of one father; in the New Testament it is without exception used for the love

[1] See my *Testaments of Love* (Eerdmans, 1981), pp. 203–211, 266–268.

uniting Christians to one another. James Denney thought that the importance of this 'is not sufficiently considered by most Christian people; who, if they looked into the matter, might find that few of their strongest affections were determined by the common faith. Is not love a strong and peculiar word to describe the feeling you cherish toward some members of the Church, brethren to you in Christ Jesus? yet love to the brethren is the very token of our right to a place in the Church for ourselves.' These words are not yet out of date.

Paul assures his friends that there is no need for him to exhort them in this matter (cf. 2 Cor. 8:1ff.), and gives as his reason that they *have been taught by God (theodidaktoi,* here only in the New Testament, though cf. Jn. 6:45) *to love each other,* which follows strikingly on the reference to the work of the Holy Spirit in the previous verse. We are reminded of Jesus' words, 'If anyone chooses to do God's will, he will find out whether my teaching comes from God' (Jn. 7:17; cf. 6:45). God is active in the sincere seeker, and specifically it is God who teaches believers to love.

10. *And in fact (kai gar)* marks an advance; it is one thing to know what to do and quite another to do it. The Thessalonians constantly practised brotherly love; the present tense in *you do (poieite)* has the full force of continuous action: 'you habitually do'. In *Macedonia* we know of churches only in Philippi, Berea and Thessalonica, but this does not mean that only these three existed. Believers in these centres would spread the gospel and missionaries like Silvanus, Timothy and Luke may have worked in other cities. Lightfoot thought it probable that churches had been established at least in the larger towns like Amphipolis and Pella. But Paul would not have them rest on their oars. He urges them *to do so more and more (perisseuein* again, as in 3:12; 4:1). Paul comes back repeatedly to the thought of the abundant life. The primary meaning here is that of abounding love, but it is fair to comment that growth and freedom from constricting restraints are integral parts of the Christian life.

D. EARNING ONE'S LIVING (4:11–12)

Following the injunction to abound in love for one another,
Paul exhorts his readers to take the lowly place. That is the way
love acts.

11. 'We urge you . . . to make it your ambition to have no
ambition!' (Phillips) brings out something of Paul's vigorous
paradox, though the exact meaning of his words is not completely clear. His verb (*philotimeomai*) in the classics meant 'to
be ambitious', but later 'to strive eagerly', 'to seek restlessly',
pointing to a whole-hearted and energetic pursuit of the object
(*cf.* Rom. 15:20; 2 Cor. 5:9, its only other New Testament occurrences). It may well have this meaning here. It is a colourful
command, whether Paul meant 'make it your ambition to be
unambitious' or 'seek restlessly to be still'.

Now come two other infinitives: *to mind your own business* and
to work with your hands. Why this stress on the virtues of the
quiet life and of steadily working at one's occupation? Some of
the Thessalonian Christians seem to have been living in idleness, depending on the charity of their fellows. They may have
reasoned that the parousia was very near; if so, would it not be
good to spend all one's time preparing people for it? Whether
that was the reason or not, it is clear that some were not working
for their living and Paul seems to have them in mind when
giving these strong injunctions to avoid the spectacular and to
work hard.

It is noteworthy that in writing to people in a Greek city he
says *work with your hands*, for Greeks despised manual labour;
they saw it as an occupation fit for slaves. But the Christians
(like the Jews) did not hesitate to insist on the dignity of manual
work (*cf.* Eph. 4:28). Some conclude that most of the Thessalonian Christians were of the artisan class, and this may well have
been so. There are few indications throughout the two Epistles
that any of them were wealthy; everything points to their coming from the lower strata of society. This is not a new command;
Paul had told them this before. His verb *told* (='commanded')
is often used of the orders of military officers. There is a ring of
authority about it.

12. Now come two reasons for earning their own living. First, *that your daily life may win the respect of outsiders*. In one sense the Christian must live without regard to the opinion of the world, for his standards are those of his Master, not those of the community in which he lives. But in another sense he must always have in mind the opinion of the world, for he must not bring discredit on the faith by being careless of appearances. The Thessalonians were distinguished by brotherly love, a fact that enabled some of them to stop working and live on the bounty of others. This was a wonderful testimony to the charity of those who provided for them, but the effect of the loafers on outsiders must have been deplorable. While believers must always be ready to help others (Gal. 6:2), believers must also shoulder their own burden (Gal. 6:5).

The second reason is that they may be independent. Paul's words may mean 'that you may have need of nothing' or 'that you may have need of no-one'; either gives a good sense. Those living on the charity of others needed to be told not to depend on men. But Paul may mean that anyone who works constantly will find ample provision for all his needs; he will have no lack of anything. Either way, he insists on the importance of being independent.

VI. PROBLEMS ASSOCIATED WITH THE PAROUSIA
(4:13 – 5:11)

Paul had clearly spoken about the parousia (see on 2:19) to good effect, and the Thessalonians were in no doubt that it would take place. But he had not dealt with all the problems associated with it, some of which obviously came up after his departure. One of them has been dealt with in the preceding section, namely the importance of earning one's living in the interval. Now Paul turns to other difficulties and treats them in a way that has left its mark on the life of the church. Rolston points out that almost every funeral service uses words from this passage.

A. BELIEVERS WHO DIED BEFORE THE PAROUSIA (4:13–18)

Some of the Thessalonians had evidently understood Paul to say that all who believed would see the parousia. Some believers had died. Did this mean that they would be at a disadvantage when the Lord came? Had they forfeited their share in the wonderful happenings of the End? Some may even have felt that these deaths discredited the whole idea of the parousia. Incidentally, the fact that such a question could be asked shows that we are dealing with an early writing, for the question was bound to arise early in the church's history.

13. *Brothers, we do not want you to be ignorant* is a Pauline formula (always with the affectionate address *brothers*); it draws attention to something important and which may be new to the readers (*cf.* Rom. 1:13; 11:25; 1 Cor. 10:1; 12:1; 2 Cor. 1:8). Paul speaks of the departed as *those who fall asleep*, where his present participle (he uses the present of this verb again only in 1 Cor. 11:30) points to an existing situation and perhaps implies a future awakening more definitely than the usual perfect would have done. Jews and even pagans sometimes spoke of death as 'sleep', but this is particularly apt for Christians, since for them the whole concept of death has been transformed,[1] a point JB misses with its 'those who have died'.

That Christians should not *grieve* like others has sometimes been taken to mean that they may sorrow but only to a lesser degree than the heathen. This seems to be straining the Greek. We need not doubt that a certain sadness at parting is natural and inevitable; but Paul 'states his precept broadly, without caring to enter into the qualifications which will suggest themselves at once to thinking men' (Lightfoot). His contrast is not between one degree of sorrow and another, but between Christian hope and pagan despair. *The rest of men, who have no hope* is a general term for the whole non-Christian world, and the characterization is apt, for pagan literature reveals a hopelessness in the face of death which is matched by the inscriptions on tombs. The contrast is exemplified in two early statements

---

[1] Our word 'cemetery' (Gk. *koimētērion*) is derived from the word used here (*koimaō*), and means 'a place of sleep'.

cited by Frame. The first is a letter of the second century which reads:

> Irene to Taonnophris and Philo, good comfort. I was as sorry and wept over the departed one as I wept for Didymas. And all things whatsoever were fitting, I did, and all mine, Epaphroditus and Thermuthion and Philion and Apollonius and Plantas. But, nevertheless, against such things one can do nothing. Therefore comfort ye one another.

Deissmann, from whom Frame takes this letter, speaks of Irene as experiencing 'the difficulty of those whose business it is to console and who have no consolation to offer' (*LAE*, p. 177). The second is from a Christian of about the same date, Aristides:

> And if any righteous man among them passes from the world, they rejoice and offer thanks to God; and they escort the body as if he were setting out from one place to another near.

There are some noble pagan utterances on immortality; but they are by no means typical, and had probably not penetrated through to ordinary people, so that the contrast in the two passages quoted may fairly be taken as representative.

14. The reason for the Christian certainty is what God has done in Christ's death and resurrection. Many hold that Paul is using traditional language here (he usually says 'Christ' rather than 'Jesus' and uses a different verb for *rose again*). Be that as it may, he is drawing attention to the central doctrines of the faith. God's action leaves no room for doubts. It is significant that he does not speak of Jesus as 'sleeping', but says he *died*. Christ endured the full horror of that death that is the wages of sin and thus transformed death for his followers into sleep. In the New Testament Christians are never said to die; they fall asleep. But Christ is not said to fall asleep (though *cf.* 1 Cor. 15:20); he died for us.[1]

The end of this verse reads 'them that sleep through Jesus God will bring with him'. There is dispute about the meaning of 'through Jesus' and whether it should be taken with the

---

[1] For death, see further my monograph, *The Wages of Sin* (Tyndale Press, 1955).

preceding or following words. Moffatt and RSV take it with *will bring*, a view that does not lack supporters. But the parallelism of the sentence is against it: this view does not face the need to show that not all the dead are meant; and in the context we read of 'the dead in Christ' (v. 16). It is moreover rather tame and even redundant to say, 'God will bring through Jesus with Jesus . . .'. It is preferable to take 'through Jesus' with 'them that sleep', even though 'sleeping through Jesus' is not an easy idea (which is why some adopt the other view). Perhaps our best understanding of it is that death has been transformed into sleep through Jesus. This is more than 'died as Christians' (NEB). For the natural man death is the antagonist that no-one can defeat, but for the Christian it is completely without terrors (*cf.* 1 Cor. 15:54–57). It is no more than sleep, and the transformation is brought about 'through Jesus'.

Some hold that those God brings *with* Jesus are being led to glory by Jesus (*e.g.* Lightfoot, Frame). But, true though this is, it does not seem to be the meaning here. Rather Paul is saying that Christ will bring them with him at his parousia. The Thessalonians do not seem to have doubted the reality of the resurrection (Paul says *will bring*, not 'will raise'); but they needed reassurance of the place in the parousia of the faithful departed. Paul gives the conclusion a touch of certainty. After 'if (omitted in NIV) we believe' we expect 'even so also we ought to believe'; but Paul states it simply as fact: 'if we believe . . . so also God will bring' (the Greek has no second 'we believe').

15. The most natural understanding of *the Lord's own word* is that Paul is quoting a saying of Jesus; but there is no saying in the Gospels exactly like this (Mt. 24:31 is perhaps the closest). There is nothing improbable in the suggestion that Paul is quoting an otherwise unrecorded saying, for there is much that is not included in the canonical Gospels (Jn. 20:30; 21:25). To the objection that such a saying must have been included in the Gospels if Jesus had said it, it is fair to retort that we do not know why the writers included some sayings and omitted others; it is not easy to think of a reason for omitting Acts 20:35, for example. Others think there was a direct revelation to Paul or some other prophet, or perhaps that this is the result of

Paul's pondering the problem in accordance with his claim to
have 'the mind of Christ' (1 Cor. 2:16; *cf.* v. 13; 2 Cor. 3:17;
Masson, 'a revelation from the Spirit received by Paul'). Rigaux
thinks it is a conclusion from the general drift of Jesus' teaching;
cf. GNB, 'What we are teaching you now is the Lord's teaching'.

Many take the words *we are still alive* to mean that Paul
expected to be alive when the Lord returns. There is nothing
unlikely in the idea, but it must be borne in mind that Paul
consistently refused to commit himself to dates; indeed, in this
very context he writes as though he did not know when it
would be (5:1–2); further, he holds that both waking and sleeping are possibilities for him and his converts (5:10). While what
he says here might fit in with the idea that he thought that he
himself would be among those who would survive to that day,
it does not establish it (*cf.* Moore, 'the certainty of this idea
arises more through its frequent assertion than its sound evidence'). The meaning may be given in Lightfoot's paraphrase:
'When I say "we," I mean those who are living, those who
survive to that day.'[1] Paul has a little-noticed habit of classing
himself with those of whom he is writing, even in activities in
which no-one would expect him to take part, like eating in
idol's temples (1 Cor. 10:22; *cf.* Rom. 3:5; Gal. 5:26, *etc.*). 'Paul
did not *teach* that the Parousia was near; but, like every true
Christian, he firmly *hoped* that it was so.'[2] If the words used here
be held to prove that Paul expected to be alive at the parousia,
then equally other words of his 'prove' that he expected to be
dead (1 Cor. 6:14; 2 Cor. 4:14; the possibility of his death appears
in 2 Cor. 5:9; Phil. 1:21–22, *etc.*). Those alive when the Lord
comes *will certainly not* (emphatic negative *ou mē*, found in Paul,
outside quotations from LXX, only in 5:3; 1 Cor. 8:13; Gal. 5:16)
precede those who have fallen asleep.

16. 'One word of command, one shout from the archangel,
one blast from the trumpet of God and the Lord himself will
come down from Heaven!' This translation of Phillips catches

---

[1] They are surely wrong who affirm that Paul thought of the parousia as imminent in his
early years, but that the idea faded in later life. Much later he still thought of the Lord's
coming as at hand (Phil. 4:5; *cf.* 1 Cor. 16:22).

[2] A. Robert and A. Feuillet, *Introduction to the New Testament* (Desclée, 1965), p. 398.

something of the vividness of Paul's words. This is the fullest description of the parousia in the New Testament, and when we reflect on the little that is said here we are warned against undue dogmatism about what will then happen. Paul's main point is that it is none other than the Lord himself who will come. The end of the age is not to be ushered in by some intermediary, but by God himself (cf. Mi. 1:3). It is awe-inspiring.

The *loud command* (*keleusma*) is used of the cry of the charioteer to his horses or the hunter to his hounds; it is the shout of the ship's master to the rowers, or of the commander to his soldiers. Always there is the ring of authority and the note of urgency. It is not said who will utter the *command*, but it may well be the Lord (cf. Jn. 5:25, 28). If not, then the *command*, the *voice* and the *trumpet call* may all be ways of referring to the same thing (Rev. 1:10 has 'a loud voice like a trumpet'). Hendriksen and others hold that the Lord utters the *command*, while the *voice* and the *trumpet call* are identical. We should reject translations that might give the impression that the Lord responds to a command (*e.g.* JB, 'At the trumpet of God, the voice of the archangel will call out the command and the Lord himself will come down'). He is in control.

Some have tried to identify the archangel, and Michael, the only archangel named in the New Testament (Jude 9), is usually favoured (Gabriel is simply an 'angel' in Lk. 1:19; there are seven 'holy angels', usually regarded as archangels, in the Apocrypha: Tobit 12:15; 1 Enoch 20:1–8). But *archangelou* lacks the article and it seems that Paul has no particular archangel in mind. Similarly *voice* has no article, so that it means 'a voice of an archangel' or perhaps 'a voice like an archangel's'. The trumpet is associated with divine activity in the Old Testament (Ex. 19:16; Is. 27:13; Joel 2:1; Zc. 9:14), and is linked elsewhere with the parousia (Mt. 24:31; 1 Cor. 15:52).

The dead in Christ (even death does not break the union; we are still *in* him) are to rise *first*, *i.e.* before the events of the next verse. It is unlikely that Paul has in mind the 'first resurrection' (Rev. 20:5), or that he is thinking of the resurrection of all men. He is simply pointing out that, far from the faithful departed missing the parousia, they will have a prominent place.

17. *After that*, believers who remain alive on earth *will be caught up with them in the clouds*. The verb *harpagēsometha* combines the ideas of force and suddenness seen in the irresistible power of God. We should not overlook the fact that believers will be caught up *with them*. There will be a reunion with Christ, but there will also be a reunion with the friends who have gone before. *Clouds* are frequently associated with divine appearances and activity (*cf.* Dn. 7:13; Mt. 24:30; Mk. 14:62; Rev. 1:7). They will *meet the Lord in the air*. The expression translated *to meet* is a kind of technical term 'for the official welcome of a newly arrived dignitary' (MM), and is very suitable in this context (*cf.* Mt. 25:6; Acts 28:15). It is a measure of the Lord's complete supremacy that he should meet his saints in such a region, for *the air* was held to be the abode of all manner of evil spirits (*cf.* Eph. 2:2). At the same time this is not anything more than a meeting-place. It seems that the Lord proceeds to the earth with his people (*cf.* 1 Cor. 6:2).

The climax comes with *we will be with the Lord for ever*. There are many points on which we should like further information. But when Paul comes to that great fact that makes everything else unimportant, he stops. There is no need (and no more) to add to that.

18. Paul calls on his readers not simply to take heart, but actively to *encourage* (see on 3:2) each other with what he has written. Whiteley sees this as very important. Paul's words are a source of continual strengthening for the believer, not a spur to fascination with the future. They convey the assurance that the power of God will never be defeated. God is supreme, and when he sees that the time has come, he will draw this age to its close and usher in the new age with the parousia. Whether we live or whether we die, we do not go beyond his power. Even in the face of death, that antagonist that no human can tame, we can remain calm and triumphant, for we know that those who sleep sleep in Jesus and that they have their place in the final scheme of things. Well might Paul call on his friends to *encourage each other with these words*.

B. THE TIME OF THE PAROUSIA (5:1–3)

It would seem that some of the Thessalonians had gone on from thinking of the place of the faithful departed at the parousia to wondering what their own position would be. If it was only the living who would have a part in the happenings of the great day, and if they were to die before it, they would fail to participate. How could they know when the end would be? The difficulty has been met already, for Paul has pointed out that the faithful departed will have an honoured place at the parousia. But he proceeds to give attention to the matter of date.

1. His first point is that they really need no instruction about the time. He had spoken of this when he was with them and he evidently counted on their having learned well what he was teaching, for he had no *need* to write on the topic. He uses two words for time, *times* and *dates* (*cf.* Acts 1:7), where the former (*chronoi*) strictly denotes time in its chronological aspect as mere succession, while the latter (*kairoi*) is used of the right time for a thing. Most scholars these days see little difference between them here, though Hendriksen refers to 'duration periods' and 'appropriate seasons' (NASB 'the times and the epochs', but there is no real justification for the last word). Paul is saying that there is no need for him to write on any aspect of the time of the parousia.

2. The emphatic opening 'yourselves' (which NIV omits) reminds the Thessalonians that the answer to this difficulty was within their grasp, if they but reflected on what they already knew. Findlay finds the word translated *very well* (*akribōs*) puzzling here; it is not a common Pauline word (elsewhere only Eph. 5:15) and Paul does not normally qualify the verb 'to know'. In the end he concludes that Paul is taking up and repeating a word used by the Thessalonians in a letter to him, and he has been followed by others. *Akribōs* does refer to accuracy, but the correct explanation here seems to be that there was nothing to add to what they already knew on the subject. There may also be a hint that their information was based ultimately on some word of the Lord (such as Mt. 24:43; Lk.

95

12:39; *cf.* 2 Pet. 3:10).

The day of the Lord is an Old Testament expression, going back to Amos 5:18. Amos, however, uses the term as already well known; he opposes the accepted understanding of it as a time of judgment for the heathen and emphasizes that Israel too will be judged. But the old idea seems to have lingered on, and many looked for the day when the enemies of Israel would be destroyed (it is always comforting to think that it is someone else that God will judge!). In the New Testament the *day* is associated with Christ as well as with the Father (Phil. 1:6, *etc.*), and it is referred to in a variety of ways. The idea of judgment remained ('the day of judgment' is one of the ways of referring to it, as in 2 Pet. 2:9), but the emphasis is on the judgment of the individual rather than on that of the nations. It is made clear that 'each of us will give an account of himself to God' (Rom. 14:12).

Paul makes his reference to its arrival more vivid with his use of the present tense 'comes' (NIV has *will come*). The comparison to the coming of a thief indicates its total unexpectedness, and this is heightened with *in the night* (only here in the New Testament do we have reference to *a thief in the night*). Leith Samuel remarks, 'if there is one thing certain about the timing of the Lord's return it is this, that we cannot be certain of the timing' (*cf.* LB, 'you know perfectly well that no one knows'). It is inevitable, but unpredictable.

3. To the generality of mankind (*people*) the parousia will be unexpected. They will be saying '*Peace and safety*' when destruction overtakes them (note the present tense, *are saying*; right at the time of the parousia they will be saying this). The idea of an imagined peace is found elsewhere (Je. 6:14; 8:11; Ezk. 13:10; Mi. 3:5). When people are in this fancied security, while they are actually saying *peace*, there will come on them *destruction*. Again the present tense ('comes') gives greater vividness. There are some coincidences of language with Luke 21:34 (*e.g.* the unusual word *aiphnidios*, 'sudden', found in these two places only in the New Testament). This kind of coincidence with Luke, where that evangelist differs from the others, perhaps indicates a connection between Paul and his friend.

We should understand *destruction* primarily in terms of separation from God (*cf.* 2 Thes. 1:9, where the same word is used), rather than of annihilation. Milligan takes it to convey 'the thought of utter and hopeless *ruin*, the loss of all that gives worth to existence'. The comparison with child-birth can be paralleled from the Old Testament (Is. 13:6–8; Je. 4:31, *etc.*), and from the teaching of Jesus (Mk. 13:8). Sometimes the point of the comparison is the pain, but here it is rather a combination of suddenness and inevitability. This latter point is underlined with the following *they will not escape*, where Paul uses the emphatic double negative *ou mē* (see on 4:15), 'they shall by no means escape' (Amp.).

C. CHILDREN OF THE DAY (5:4–11)

In strong contrast with the fate of these unbelievers is the situation of those in Christ (in v. 4 *you* is emphatic). The apostle makes use of a word-play: the day of the Lord passes over into the day (or light) in which Christians live. Paul develops the thought of living as children of the day.

4. He expresses his confidence that the Thessalonians will not find themselves in the calamitous situation he has just outlined. *You, brothers* (note the affectionate address as in v. 1), *are not in darkness*, which means more than 'you are not ignorant'. The present world is a place of darkness (2 Cor. 6:14; Eph. 6:12), out of which Christ has saved the believer (Col. 1:13); God has made the light shine in our hearts and given us knowledge of his glory 'in the face of Christ' (2 Cor. 4:6). Since the Thessalonian Christians have come into the light of Christ they have passed from the possibility of destruction. Paul seems to be carrying on the metaphor of the thief coming suddenly in the night, though we should notice that some MSS have the reading 'as day overtakes thieves' (*kleptas* as against *kleptēs*), a reading accepted by Lightfoot, Milligan, Frame and others, largely on the grounds that scribes would not alter the accepted reading to this one, but they would be greatly tempted to conform this one to the other. Most textual critics, however, accept the reading behind NIV; the attestation of the variant is limited and it seems to be a mechanical corruption, the ending of *kleptēs* being conformed to that of the nearby *hymas*.

5. There are both positive and negative reasons why the day should not surprise them. Positively they are all *sons of the light* (*cf.* Lk. 16:8). In the Semitic idiom to be a 'son' of something is to be characterized by that thing (*e.g.* 'a son of strength' means 'a strong man'); 'light' is the distinguishing characteristic of believers. This means more than being 'in light' and points to the transformation that Christ has made in them. *Sons of the day* (here only in the New Testament) is similar to *sons of the light*, for day is the region of light; but it is not a simple repetition, for it looks back to 'the day of the Lord' (v. 2). They will participate in the triumph of that great day; they belong to that great day; they will have the fulfilment of their being when that great day comes.

There is a significant change from *you* to *we* as Paul associates himself with his converts in the need to live uprightly, as those who will share in the blessings of the parousia. *We* (*i.e.* 'we who believe'), he says, do not belong to the sphere of *night* or *darkness*. *Night* stands over against *day* and perhaps points to the period (they belong not to the *night* of the present age, but to 'the day of the Lord'), while *darkness* (over against *light*) is the condition of opposition to God.

6. *So then* (*ara oun*; used only by Paul in the New Testament) is a strong expression for a necessary logical inference, and introduces an inescapable conclusion. Paul uses a different word for *asleep* (*katheudō*) from that in 4:13–15 (*koimaō*), and, while there is not a great deal of difference between the two, it may not be without significance that the one used here is some-times used of moral indifference (Mk. 13:36; Eph. 5:14). It is the condition natural to the enemies of Christ, for they belong to the night. They are here referred to as *others* (*hoi loipoi*, 'the rest') , *i.e.* all non-Christians.

By contrast, Christians are exhorted, *let us be alert and self-controlled*. The first verb is concerned with mental alertness, being watchful for the parousia (*cf.* Mt. 24:42–43; 25:13; Mk.

13:34–37, *etc.*), while the second has a moral emphasis and is used to condemn all kinds of excess. It can be used of the avoidance of alcoholic intoxication, but it seems to be used metaphorically here (as with *asleep, etc.*), for there is no indication that the Thessalonians were addicted to drunkenness and thus in need of an exhortation to sobriety in the literal sense. Rather Paul is saying that Christians must live temperately, avoiding excess of all kinds; they must live balanced lives.

7. The kind of conduct Paul is opposing belongs to the night, not the day, and he has already pointed out that his readers are 'sons of day'. The expressions used here are not metaphorical; Paul is simply saying that night is the time when people sleep and night is the time when they get drunk (*cf.* Acts 2:15). He uses two different verbs in connection with the latter, the first of which means literally 'to get drunk' (in the passive, used here; the active means 'to make drunk'), and the second 'to be drunk'. But there is no stress on the difference; Paul is using them virtually as synonyms, the variation being purely stylistic.

8. *But* (in contrast with such people) *since we belong to the day, let us be self-controlled. We* is the emphatic *hēmeis*; it is not mankind in general but 'we Christians', we who belong to the day, of whom he writes. He repeats his injunction to sobriety, and this forms a transition to the idea of the armour of the Christian soldier. The connectiom of thought is not obvious, but there is a similar sequence in Romans 13:12–13. Perhaps 'the mention of vigilance suggested the idea of a sentry armed and on duty' (Lightfoot). Paul has an aorist participle (*putting on*), which suggests the taking of a decisive, once-for-all step. The metaphor of the Christian's armour attracted Paul and he uses it a number of times (Rom. 13:12–13; 2 Cor. 6:7; 10:4; Eph. 6:13–17). The details are not always the same, which is a warning against pressing the metaphor too closely. Thus in Ephesians the breastplate is righteousness and faith is the shield, while neither hope nor love is mentioned. The idea probably goes back to Isaiah 59:17, where Yahweh is depicted as a warrior armed.

Once again we meet the great triad of faith, hope and love (see on 1:3), and again hope comes last with a certain emphasis, which is natural in a letter that puts such stress on hope. In each case there is an appositional genitive, so that *faith and love* are the *breastplate*, and *the hope of salvation* is the *helmet*. Whiteley remarks that *hope* is 'not "mere" hope, as often in modern speech, but a sure and certain expectation'. We should not miss the note of certainty.

Salvation is the general and inclusive term for the whole great work of Christ for us, of which redemption and the like are aspects. The link with *hope* shows that here the future, eschatological consummation of all things is especially in mind. The hope that rests on what Christ has done and reaches forward to the final unfolding of all that salvation means is indeed a helmet for the Christian, warding off the world's hard knocks.

9. The reason for our 'hope of salvation' is that God has appointed (*etheto*) it. The verb is 'somewhat vague' (Milligan), being not nearly as precise, for example, as 'predestined' (Rom. 8:29–30); but it clearly rests our salvation on the divine initiative. It is due to God that believers are brought into salvation.

God did not appoint us to *wrath* (again some translations come short of the meaning, as JB, 'the Retribution'; NEB, 'the terrors of judgement'; but Paul sees God as personally active in opposing evil; see on 1:10). Salvation is salvation *from* as well as salvation *unto*. As Heinrich Vogel puts it, 'whoever thinks he can smile at God's wrath will never praise him eternally for his grace'.[1] One of the things that gave salvation so full a meaning for New Testament Christians was that they were sure of the wrath of God and had a deep gratitude to Christ for saving them from it. In modern times some take Christianity lightly because they have emptied the *wrath* of its content. To banish the wrath of God from the scene is to rob life of a good deal of its serious purpose.

The expression *to receive salvation* (*eis peripoiēsin sotērias*) may mean 'for the acquiring of salvation' (JB 'to win salvation'), or, taking the former word passively, 'for the adoption of salvation' (Lightfoot). Passages may be found to support either (the active sense: 2 Thes. 2:14; Heb. 10:39; the passive: Eph. 1:14; 1 Pet.

---

[1] H. Vogel, *The Iron Ration of a Christian* (SCM, 1941), p. 102.

2:9). The former meaning seems natural, but it is objected that to some extent it makes our salvation a matter of human activity, whereas Paul consistently sees God as bringing us salvation. Bruce, however, finds the second meaning 'strained' and it is difficult to disagree. Paul is here speaking of salvation in its eschatological aspect and the point is that that is yet to be 'acquired' (cf. Rom. 13:11). This does not mean that it is obtained by human effort, and Paul immediately goes on to say that it is obtained *through our Lord Jesus Christ*. Whatever activity be ascribed to the believer, salvation is God's gift through Christ (for the divine and the human in salvation cf. Eph. 2:8–10; Phil. 2:12–13).

10. The way salvation was accomplished comes out in the words *He died for us*. This is the only place in the Thessalonian letters where Christ's death is explicitly said to be *for us*. It cannot be inferred that Paul was feeling his way to a theology, for at the very time that he wrote this letter he was preaching a gospel where the cross was central (1 Cor. 1:23–24; 2:1–2; 15:3–7). Indeed, it is difficult to think that he could have alluded to Christ's death in this fashion unless it was already a familiar, non-controversial topic for the Thessalonians (cf. 2:15; 4:14). In these letters Paul is occupied primarily with other matters, and accordingly does not deal at length with doctrines accepted by all. Lightfoot finds it important that, though Paul's concern is with other matters, he yet mentions this topic. It shows that it was present to his mind even when he was busied with other things. And this within twenty years of Jesus' death.

The purpose of Christ's death for us is our union with him, and it is significant that this central Pauline concept is present thus early in his ministry. Union with Christ means entering a new relationship so enduring in its effects that even death cannot affect it. *Whether we are awake or asleep* means 'whether we live or die' (cf. Rom. 14:8); it is physical life and physical death that are in mind, not the ethical use as in verse 6 (though Thomas thinks of the ethical use here also). The words are a further reassurance for those experiencing the difficulty treated in 4:13–18. Whatever be our state when Christ comes again, we will live with him.

11. Paul's words about the parousia come to a close with an exhortation to help one another (cf. 4:18). *Therefore* (dio) means 'on account of the things laid down in the preceding passage'; it is probable that everything from 4:13 onwards is included. The concept of edification (building up) is one that Paul uses often. The verb *oikodomeō* is not uncommon in the New Testament in its usual sense of building (e.g. Mt. 7:24, 26). Jesus used it of building his church (Mt. 16:18), and it is applied to the growth of the church (Acts 9:31). But in Paul's hands both the verb and the cognate nouns are in frequent use in the sense 'edify', and this in both his early and later writings. It perhaps reaches its climax with the thought of believers being built up into a temple of the Holy Spirit (cf. 1 Cor. 3:9–17, Eph. 2:21–22).

Paul rounds off the section with a tactful *just as in fact you are doing*. He is always ready to give credit where credit is due. His purpose here is to exhort and encourage the brothers in the right way, not to rebuke them.

VII. GENERAL EXHORTATIONS (5:12–22)

As his letter draws to its close Paul mentions some other matters briefly. Firstly, there is the attitude of church members to their leaders. The most probable reading of the situation is that, in the prevailing restlessness, the leaders of the church had rebuked some of the members, possibly those who had stopped working. Their exhortation was perhaps not as tactful as it might have been, and it seems not to have been received meekly. Paul thus addresses the church at large, urging members to have a proper respect for their leaders (12–13), then, still addressing the church at large, but clearly with the leaders specially in mind, he counsels consideration and patience (14–15).

12. *Now we ask you* is the tone of respectful request; while *brothers* shows that the request is addressed to the whole church. *Respect* translates *eidenai*, a verb which means 'know' and is rarely if ever used in this way elsewhere. Most understand it in some such way as 'appreciate' or 'respect', but Moore thinks that 'acknowledge' (NEB) 'is more exact'.

The three following participles are preceded by a common article which indicates that it is one group of persons and not three that is in mind. This points to elders, who alone would exercise the triple function. Frame objects, for 'we are in the period of informal and voluntary leadership', and many follow him. But elders were appointed from quite early times (Acts 11:30; 14:23), and, from the model of the Jewish synagogue, elders are to be expected even in very young churches (once an assembly of Christians is called a synagogue, Jas. 2:2). It may be possible for an organization to exist without office-bearers of any kind; but it is far from usual, and such evidence as we have does not indicate that the early church made the attempt. We do not know the precise functions of the early elders and at this time these may not have been defined with any exactness. But this passage shows that there were recognized leaders, whatever functions they performed and whether they were called 'elders' or not ('your teachers', JB, is too definite). Rigaux sees a reference to presbyters.

Of the three terms employed *work hard* is quite general; it properly means laborious toil (*cf.* the use of the corresponding noun in 1:3). Some function of leadership is clearly implied in the expression *who are over you*. The verb (*proistēmi*) is used of informal leaderships of various kinds, but it is also used of officials, as the papyri plainly show (see MM). Bo Reicke sees a reference here to people whose task 'is in large measure that of pastoral care' (*TDNT*, vi, p. 702). Hort thinks it 'morally impossible' that this can be the title of an office, but he can still say, 'It can hardly be doubted that Elders are meant, though no title is given.'[1] The words *in the Lord* go with this verb and this makes it clear that it is spiritual authority that is in mind. The third participle, *admonish*, is found in the New Testament only in the Pauline writings and in a speech of Paul's in Acts 20:31. 'It denotes the word of admonition which is designed to correct while not provoking or embittering' (J. Behm, *TDNT*, iv, p. 1021). It seems to carry a suggestion of blame for wrongdoing (*cf.* 'warn those who are idle', v. 14) and is aimed at correcting

---

[1] F. J. A. Hort, *The Christian Ecclesia* (Macmillan, 1897), p. 126.

the wrong. Best sees it as addressed to the will rather than the mind.

13. The verb *hēgeomai* is not found elsewhere in the sense 'hold in high regard' (it means 'consider', 'deem', as in 2 Thes. 3:15, 'regard'), but in this context NIV seems correct. Again, it is not certain whether we should take *in love* with the verb or with the adverb, *i.e.* whether the meaning is 'hold them in love, and do it exceedingly' (with love the primary idea), or 'esteem them highly' (with 'in love' a somewhat loose addition). Whatever our decision it is clear that the two ideas of high esteem and love are present (*cf.* GNB, 'Treat them with the greatest respect and love'). Some translations have 'affection' (*e.g.* NEB, JB), but *agapē* is more than this. The adverb *hyperekperissou* is a very forceful word (see on 3:10), called by Findlay a 'triple Pauline intensive' meaning 'beyond-exceeding-abundantly' (*CGT*). Paul then is making a strong plea for the leaders to be held in the highest regard, and this, not for reasons of personal eminence or office, but *because of their work*. They 'work hard' (v. 12) and it is the duty of the rank and file to do all they can to forward that work. Leaders can never do their best work when they are subject to carping criticism from those who should be their followers. Good leaders need good followers.

Lightfoot thinks that Paul glides off at this point 'from special precepts into a general and comprehensive one'. But it is better to see the same situation as dictating the next words. It seems clear that the leaders in the church had not been sufficiently highly regarded and their authority had been resisted. In all probability they had not exercised their authority as tactfully as they might have done, and in this situation the injunction *Live in peace with each other* is very much in place. The exhortation applies to all (*each other*), including the leaders; it is not simply a counsel of submission on the part of the rank and file. The pursuit of peace is an Old Testament injunction (Ps. 34:14), and one taken seriously in the New Testament (Mk. 9:50; Rom. 12:18; 2 Cor. 13:11).

14. The counsel given in this verse is best understood as applying specially to the leaders. But it is not specifically addressed to them, but to the church as a whole. This means that, while the officers have a special responsibility in the matters named, the duties are not confined to them; they are the responsibility in due measure of all believers. All must be ready to help the *idle*, the *timid*, and the *weak*.

Warn translates the verb rendered 'admonish' in verse 12 (where see comment). *Idle* (*ataktous*) is a military term for the soldier who does not keep in rank. It is found only here in the New Testament and the corresponding verb and adverb are confined to 2 Thessalonians (3:6, 7, 11). Evidently the problem was unusual and confined to the Thessalonians. G. Delling says that the word group 'characterises a man as one who sets himself outside the necessary and given order' (*TDNT*, viii, p. 48). Milligan has a long note in which he shows that in the papyri these words are used of being 'idle'. Frame quotes a later letter from Milligan with further supporting evidence, but he himself thinks it is not idleness as such but culpable idleness ('loafing') that is meant. Such conduct is not to be tolerated in a Christian community.

For *encourage* see on 2:11–12. The *timid* (*oligopsychous*; here only in the New Testament) may be those who naturally lack courage or those who had become discouraged by particular circumstances (like believers becoming despondent when friends died before the parousia, 4:13). Bruce sees the meaning as the 'inadequate and diffident', Best as the 'worried'. Such need encouragement from their Christian comrades. The *weak* must refer to the weak spiritually, not physically (*cf.* Rom. 14; 1 Cor. 8). The verb *antechesthe* (*help*) is used of holding on to something, cleaving to a person (*cf.* Lk. 16:13). The weak need to feel that they are not alone and strong Christians should 'hold on to them' and give them the support they require.

Following the injunctions for particular classes we have one for *everyone*. The verb *makrothymeō*, *be patient*, is the opposite of *oxothymeō*, 'to be short-tempered' and gives the idea of steady patience. Impatience is easy (for good reasons as well as bad), but for the Christian the rule is long-suffering, and that towards all, not just Christians. This is part of what love means (1 Cor. 13:4).

15. Paul changes from the second to the third person, 'see that no-one renders . . .'. Not only has each one a responsibility for his own conduct, the whole community has a responsibility for each of its members. This applies to leaders, but also to others; every Christian must give attention to the conduct of the whole group.

The prohibition of retaliation is found elsewhere with the same Greek verb and the same words *wrong for wrong* (Rom. 12:17; 1 Pet. 3:9; NIV has 'evil for evil' in both). It may go back to some saying of Jesus (*cf.* Mt. 5:43–44), or to the Old Testament (Pr. 25:21). Faced with opposition from both Jews and Gentiles, retaliation must have been a strong temptation to the Thessalonians. But Christian teaching is not meant to be applied only when circumstances are easy. Christianity is a robust faith, empowered with a divine dynamic, and is to be lived out even under the most trying circumstances.

The negative is followed by the positive, *always try to be kind* (or 'good', RSV; *agathon*). This last word stands over against 'evil' and thus denotes what is helpful to others rather than the pursuit of the moral ideal. It is the attitude of returning blessing for cursing, of being actively friendly in the face of hostility. This is more than occasional small acts of kindness; it is a life lived in an attitude of Christian love (*always try*). The verb *try* (*diōkete*) means something like 'pursue vigorously' and is the usual word for 'persecute'. It is interesting to find Paul the 'persecutor' (1 Tim. 1:13) using this strong term for the Christian duty of doing good (*cf.* the pursuit of love, 1 Cor. 14:1; righteousness, 1 Tim. 6:11; peace, Heb. 12:14). It is a duty to be exercised within the brotherhood (*to each other*), but also to outsiders (*to everyone else*). Christian love is not to be restricted; it is to be our attitude to all.

16. The injunction *Be joyful always* is at first sight a little surprising coming from one who had had to suffer as much and as continually as Paul. But he learned that affliction and deep joy may go together (2 Cor. 6:10; 12:10), and he rejoiced in tribulations (Rom. 5:3; Col. 1:24; *cf.* Acts 5:41; 16:25). So he counsels perpetual rejoicing to a suffering church (*cf.* 1:6). The note of joy is often struck in his other letter to a Macedonian church, that to the Philippians (*cf*. Phil. 4:4). Indeed, few things about the New Testament church are more remarkable than this continual stress on joy. From an outward point of view there was little to make believers rejoice. But they were 'in Christ'; they had learned the truth of his words, 'no-one will take away your joy' (Jn. 16:22). Now joy is part of the fruit of the Spirit (Gal. 5:22; *cf*. Rom. 14:17); it is not something Christians work up out of their own resources. The various derivatives of joy occur with startling frequency throughout the New Testament. The word for 'grace', for example, is from this root, as are one of the words for 'to forgive', one for 'to give thanks', and another for 'gifts of the Spirit'. New Testament Christianity is permeated with the spirit of holy joy.

17. 'It is not in the moving of the lips, but in the elevation of the heart to God, that the essence of prayer consists' (Lightfoot), and it is this that enables us to put into practice the injunction *pray continually* (*cf*. Lk. 18:1; Rom. 12:12; Eph. 6:18). It is not possible for us to spend all our time with the words of prayer on our lips, but it is possible for us to be all our days in the spirit of prayer, realizing our dependence on God for all we have and are, being conscious of his presence with us wherever we may be, and yielding ourselves continually to him to do his will. Such an inward state will of course find expression from time to time in verbal prayer (notice the frequent ejaculatory prayers throughout Paul's letters; prayer was so natural to Paul that it inevitably found its way into his correspondence).

18. Paul had learned that 'in all things God works for the good of those who love him' (Rom. 8:28). Even in our difficulties and trials God is teaching valuable lessons (Rom. 5:3–5), and they are to be welcomed and used accordingly. This conviction of the divine sovereignty and providence leads to the command, *give thanks in all circumstances*. It may not be easy to see the bright side of a particular trial, but if God is over all, then his hand is in that trial; his own cannot but recognize his goodness and make their thanksgiving. Perhaps we should notice that *in all circumstances* is not quite the same as 'at every time' (the two are differentiated in 2 Cor. 9:8).

For this is God's will almost certainly refers to all three injunctions, even though *this* is singular. They form a unity and belong together. *Will* has no article; as in 4:3 it is not the totality of the divine will that is in mind. God would have us do other things, but this triad is certainly part of his will for us. The addition *in Christ Jesus* is characteristically Pauline. God's will is made known in Christ, and it is in Christ that we are given the dynamic that enables us to carry out that divine will.

19. The verb *put out* (AV 'quench') is the proper word for putting out a fire (*cf.* Mk. 9:48, *etc.*); it is an appropriate word to use of the Spirit, whose coming was with 'what seemed to be tongues of fire' (Acts 2:3; *cf.* Mt. 3:11), and who brings warmth and light to the Christian life. The negative *mē* with the present imperative may be a command to cease from something already in progress (though Bruce has his doubts; he prefers the thought of habitually refraining from the activity).

Most commentators take the injunction to refer to the ecstatic gifts of the Spirit (such as speaking in tongues), and see a contrast with the situation in Corinth. There Paul had occasion to curb an exaggerated dependence on the gifts; here, it is said, there is the opposite; some of the more conservative believers were frowning on enthusiasts who eagerly pursued the more spectacular gifts. This is possible, but the evidence is not strong and the words are very general. 'Do not grieve the Holy Spirit of God' (Eph. 4:30) is a similar general statement, and most agree that there is no reference in that passage to the ecstatic gifts. It is possible to 'quench' the Spirit (or to 'grieve' him) by such matters as those mentioned earlier in the Epistle – despondency, idleness, immorality and the like – and it is best to take the word in such a general sense. Masson acutely points out that the words refer to the Spirit, not the inspired!

20. One manifestation of the Spirit's activity is singled out for special mention, *do not treat prophecies with contempt* (*cf.* 1 Cor. 14:1). Like some Corinthians, some Thessalonians may have thought more of spectacular gifts, like tongues, than of prophecy (see 1 Cor. 14), and Paul may be seeking to redress the balance. But there is no evidence, and a more likely conjecture is that there had been prophetic outbursts in connection with second advent speculations. At all times in history the two have tended to go together, and at all times one result has been that those not caught up in the advent speculation tend to regard prophecy lightly. Some of the Thessalonians seem to have been over-enthusiastic in their views on the parousia and others seem to have rebuked them rather tactlessly (see on vv. 12ff.). There is nothing improbable in the idea that, in the process, they had come to look slightingly on prophecy.

The New Testament clearly regards the prophets as import-ant. They are classed with apostles (Eph. 2:20; 3:5), and, more formally, ranked second to them (1 Cor. 12:28; Eph. 4:11). Prophecy is the gift of God (1 Cor. 12:28; Eph. 4:11), or of the Spirit (1 Cor. 12:10–11). Commentators regularly point out that prophets were forth-tellers rather than fore-tellers; their char-acteristic function seems to have been exhortation (Acts 15:32, and *cf.* the notable discussion in 1 Cor. 14, especially vv. 29–40). Essentially the prophet was someone who could say, 'Thus saith the Lord'. But it should not be overlooked that this might, and sometimes did, involve foretelling the future (Acts 11:27–28; 21:10–11).

21. Paul does not advocate an uncritical acceptance of any-thing uttered by one who claimed to be a prophet (the verse begins with *de*, 'but', which NIV omits). He proceeds *Test every-thing* (*cf.* Phil. 1:9–10). This is a general precept, not one limited to testing spiritual gifts (as NEB 'bring them all to the test'), though it has its application to that problem. The verb is *doki-mazō*, which is often used of testing metals, and may derive from this practice. It comes to mean testing in general and has the secondary meaning of approving as a result of test. Here it plainly means 'avoid gullibility', 'apply spiritual tests to all that claims to be from God'.

Most of the early Greek commentators connect the words with a saying attributed to Jesus, 'Be ye approved money changers.'[1] If this is a genuine saying of Jesus (and the evidence makes it likely), it may have been in Paul's mind as he wrote

---

[1] See the discussion in J. Jeremias, *Unknown Sayings of Jesus* (SPCK, 1957), pp. 89–93.

these words. At any rate he is advocating the same kind of attitude; M. R. James holds that his words 'are really a comment on the saying, and show its meaning'.[1] But it is not enough to apply the test: that which the test approves must be held fast. *Hold on to the good*, writes Paul, and his word for *good* (*kalos*) is sometimes used of coins that ring true; they are genuine as compared with counterfeit coin. The Thessalonians should not take all claims at face value; they should test them and hold fast only (but always) to what is good.

22. They should also *Avoid every kind of evil*. The preposition 'from' is used to emphasize the complete separation of the believer 'from' evil (LB 'Keep away from every kind of evil'; there is a similar 'from' in 4:3, referring to unchastity). There is some doubt about the meaning of *eidous* (*kind*), and again whether *evil* is a noun or an adjective. Not much depends on the latter point, for, as Calvin pointed out, the meaning is much the same. *Eidos* may mean the outward appearance (Lk. 3:22, 'form'), or 'sort, species, kind', which appears to be the meaning here. Some think it means 'semblance' (AV 'appearance'), but this sense is not attested and in any case it seems unlikely that Paul would be concerned only with the outward appearance. Our choice seems to be between 'every visible form of evil' (with no notion of unreality) and 'every kind of evil'. The use of the word elsewhere in the New Testament favours the former, but there are enough examples of the term in the latter sense in the papyri (see MM) to make it quite possible, and in view of the context, this seems to be the right meaning. Paul is urging his friends to avoid evil of every kind (*cf.* Rom. 12:9).

The change from 'the good' (v. 21) to *every kind of evil* may well be significant. The good is one, but evil is manifold; it is to be avoided in all its forms.

VIII. CONCLUSION (5:23–28)

Paul concluded the first main section of the letter with a prayer referring to the parousia (3:11–13), and he does the same now.

[1] M. R. James, *The Apocryphal New Testament* (Oxford, 1926), p. 35.

23. *De* (omitted in NIV) has adversative force, 'but'. The conduct Paul has been advocating is impossible in human strength, *but* Paul's prayer directs the readers to the source of the power that would alone enable them to live in this way. He speaks of God as *the God of peace*, as he often does towards the end of his letters (*cf.* Rom. 15:33; 16:20; 2 Cor. 13:11; Phil. 4:9; 2 Thes. 3:16). *Peace* (see on 1:1) is spiritual prosperity in the widest sense; it is so characteristic of God to bestow this gift that he is called *the God of peace*.

The prayer is that this God will *sanctify you through and through*. There is a manward aspect of sanctification, in that we are called on to consecrate ourselves to the doing of God's will. But the power manifest in the sanctified life is not human but divine, and Paul's prayer reflects this truth. In the deepest sense our sanctification is the work of God in us; it may be ascribed to the Son (Eph. 5:26), or to the Spirit (Rom. 15:16), but in any case it is divine. *Through and through* (*holoteleis*, here only in the New Testament) combines the ideas of wholeness and completeness; Lightfoot sees the meaning, 'may He sanctify you so that ye be entire'.

The second part of the prayer runs, *May your whole spirit, soul and body be kept blameless.* . . . This is sometimes used as an argument for a trichotomous view of man (*e.g.* Thomas), as against a dichotomous view, but this is probably unjustified (*cf.* Mk. 12:30 for a fourfold division and 1 Cor. 7:34 for a twofold one). Paul is not analysing the nature of man, but uttering a fervent prayer that the entire man be preserved. *Cf.* Milligan, the threefold petition is 'for man's whole being, whether on its immortal, its personal, or its bodily side'.

That the unity of man is being emphasized is indicated by the fact that both the verb and the adjective *whole* are singular, though they apply to all three. *Whole* (*holoklēron*) is in the predicate and not the attributive position, and strictly means 'may your spirit *etc.* be preserved whole' (*cf.* RSV 'be kept sound'). The word means 'complete in all its parts'. It is used in LXX of stone for the altar (Dt. 27:6), and Philo and Josephus use it of sacrificial victims. It is thus possible that Paul is thinking of the presentation of the whole man as a living sacrifice (as in Rom. 12:1). The prayer is that the whole person be *kept blameless*, the latter word being found in this Epistle only in the New Testament. It is found also in the inscriptions on some tombs at Thessalonica (Milligan).

These Epistles have a deep interest in the second coming and fittingly the prayer concludes with a reference to it. The prayer is not only that they may be kept until the coming, but that *at* (*en*) *the coming* they may be preserved, *i.e.* in all that will then happen, including the judgment with all that that implies.

24. The prayer is offered in the certainty that it will be answered, a certainty that arises because God *is faithful* (*cf.* 1 Cor. 1:9; 10:13; 2 Cor. 1:18; 2 Thes. 3:3; 2 Tim. 2:13; Heb. 10:23; 11:11). *Cf.* Chrysostom: 'This happens not from my prayers, he says, but from the purpose with which he called you' (cited in Frame). God is *the one who calls you*, where the timeless present participle (not 'called') draws attention to God in his capacity as Caller. This is followed by an unusual absolute use of the verb *do* (there is no *it* in the Greek). This puts the emphasis on action, on 'doing', and this is strengthened by the 'also'. The faithful Caller will also act.

25. We see a very human Paul in this request to his friends (he calls them *Brothers*) for prayer (see also Rom. 15:30; Eph. 6:19; Col. 4:3-4; 2 Thes. 3:1-2, and *cf.* Phil. 1:19; Heb. 13:18). Although he had great gifts and was of undoubted eminence in the church, he needed the prayers of his friends.

26. 'In the ancient world one kissed the hand, breast, knee, or foot of a superior, and the cheek of a friend. Herodotus mentions kissing the lips as a custom of the Persians. Possibly from them it came to the Jews.'[1] In New Testament times it might be expected from a host to a guest (Lk. 7:45), and it was a gesture of goodwill which made Judas's kiss so heinous (Lk. 22:48). Not much is known of kissing in the early church, but it is usually held that men kissed men and women women, and that the kiss was on the cheek. But Tertullian (at the end of the second century) speaks of a wife exchanging a kiss with 'any

---

[1] Crawford H. Toy, *A Critical and Exegetical Commentary on the Book of Proverbs* (T. & T. Clark, 1899), p. 453, n.

one of the brothers' (*To His Wife*, ii. 4). The New Testament does not connect it with liturgical practices, but the kiss would naturally be exchanged when Christians came together to worship, and it is not surprising that in time it came to be included in the service of Holy Communion (though not confined to this). Clement of Alexandria complains of those who 'make the churches resound' with their kissing, and goes on to say, 'the shameless use of a kiss . . . occasions foul suspicions and evil reports' (*Instructor* iii.12). Such abuses led to restriction and, for example, the *Apostolic Constitutions* (4th century, but containing older material) direct men to kiss men and women women.

Paul means 'Give all the brothers a kiss from me' (*cf.* 'My love to all of you in Christ Jesus', 1 Cor. 16:24); it is his warm greeting to his Thessalonian friends. There are other references to such a 'holy kiss' (Rom. 16:16; 1 Cor. 16:20; 2 Cor. 13:12), and to a 'kiss of love' (1 Pet. 5:14).

Much is sometimes made of the fact that Paul says *Greet all the brothers* and not simply 'Greet one another' (Introduction, p. 32). But probably no great emphasis should be laid on *all*, for the word is not in an emphatic position. If Paul is not directing them how to greet one another but sending his own greeting to the church, it is natural for him to refer to *all the brothers*.

27. The strength of the language here is surprising. *I charge you before the Lord* means 'I put you on your oath as Christians', the verb being *enorkizō*, apparently a strengthened form of *horkizō* (we would expect something like 'See that this letter is read to all'). The use of 'I' (not 'we') may also be significant, though it perhaps means no more than at this point Paul took up the pen to add a few words himself.

It is not easy to explain such a strong charge. Some see in it a reference to a divided church, with some members not wishing to have others hear the letter, or perhaps not wanting to hear it themselves. But, while there were some tensions in the church (as we have noted in the commentary), there is nothing to indicate that the church was as seriously divided as this. We cannot imagine Paul praising it so highly if it were so seriously split. It is much the same with the suggestion that this is one of the earliest Epistles and the custom of reading it to all was not yet established. If this were all, there seems no need of 'I adjure'! Lightfoot suggests that Paul may have had a presentiment 'that a wrong use might be made of his name and authority. Such a suspicion was entirely justified by subsequent occurrences (2 Thess. ii. 2).' Perhaps. But it is dangerous to appeal to possible presentiments to explain passages we find difficult.

The best explanation seems to lie in the intense desire of Paul and the Thessalonians to see each other again, together with the impossibility of that happening in the prevailing circumstances. Paul uses strong words to make sure that his message comes before everybody and is plainly seen to be meant to come before everybody. This makes clear that his continued absence was not his fault. Possibly also he is moved by special concern for the bereaved who might be absent when the letter was read. He makes it certain that they will not miss the comfort he is sending them.

The word *read* (*anagnōsthēnai*) means 'read' or 'read aloud'. Some hold that reading was always aloud in antiquity, but Lake and Cadbury maintain that it is 'surely incredible that educated Greeks and Romans had not learned to read silently' (on Acts 8:30). Milligan cites examples of the use of the word in the sense of reading as well as of reading aloud. Here it clearly means 'read aloud'. Reading during public worship is not implied, though in time this became usual, and Paul's letters were read in church as sacred Scripture.

28. Instead of the customary secular ending 'Farewell' (*errōso, errōsthe*), Paul always has a prayer for *grace*. This verse is the typical form, which was sometimes expanded (*e.g.* the Trinitarian form, 2 Cor. 13:14), sometimes shortened (Col. 4:18; and the Pastorals). It was Paul's habit to pen the concluding portion himself after an amanuensis had written the main body of the letter (2 Thes. 3:17). The precise point at which he took the pen seems to have varied (*cf.* Gal. 6:11); the use of the first person singular makes it likely that in this letter it was by verse 27 at any rate.

2 THESSALONIANS: ANALYSIS

I. GREETING (1:1–2)

II. PRAYER (1:3–12)
    a. Thanksgiving (1:3–5)
    b. Divine judgment (1:6–10)
    c. Paul's prayer (1:11–12)

III. THE PAROUSIA (2:1–12)
    a. The day of the Lord not yet present (2:1–2)
    b. The great rebellion (2:3–12)
        1. The man of lawlessness (2:3–10a)
        2. The man of lawlessness's followers (2:10b–12)

IV. THANKSGIVING AND ENCOURAGEMENT (2:13–17)
    a. Thanksgiving (2:13–15)
    b. Prayer for the converts (2:16–17)

V. THE FAITHFULNESS OF GOD (3:1–5)
    a. Request for prayer (3:1–2)
    b. God's faithfulness (3:3–5)

VI. GODLY DISCIPLINE (3:6–15)
    a. The disorderly (3:6–13)
    b. The disobedient (3:14–15)

VII. CONCLUSION (3:16–18)

2 THESSALONIANS: COMMENTARY

I. GREETING (1:1–2)

1–2. The address is exactly the same as that in the first Epistle, except that *our* is included with *Father*: it is God as Father of believers, rather than as the Father of the Lord Jesus Christ. The greeting is also the same as that in the first letter, but with the addition of the words that follow *peace* in verse 2 (NIV has them in the margin). These words are probably absent from the first Epistle but genuine here. This longer form became usual in Paul's Epistles, being found in each one except 1 Thessalonians (and with the omission of 'and the Lord Jesus Christ' from Colossians). The source of the Christian's *grace and peace* is no less than God himself. Paul often links *grace* with Christ and *peace* with the Father, but in his greetings he makes no distinction. Notice the close linking of *God our Father* with *the Lord Jesus Christ* (there is but one *apo*).

II. PRAYER (1:3–12)

A. THANKSGIVING (1:3–5)

3. As in the first Epistle, Paul begins with thanksgiving for the Christian graces evident in his converts. He has used some flattering expressions about them in that letter, and it is not unlikely that in a subsequent communication they had modestly disclaimed being worthy of such praise. Paul insists that his praise was in order: *We ought always to thank God for you*. Some have seen in this a rather stiff and formal approach, quite different from that in the first Epistle, but this is refuted by the warm expressions that follow. The Greek *opheilomen, we ought,* conveys the idea of personal obligation (*dei,* often used in similar contexts, would signify a compulsion arising out of external circumstances). *And rightly so* is not simply a repetition of the same thought, but means 'It is no more than you deserve'. Paul insists that the merits of the Thessalonians are real, and that this imposes on him an obligation to recognize the fact.

He gives thanks for two points, the growth of the converts' *faith* and the abundance of their *love,* two matters about which he had prayed (1 Thes. 3:10, 12). He had been anxious about their faith (1 Thes. 3:5–7) but now gives thanks for its vigorous growth. His verb *hyperauxanei* (only here in the New Testament) gives the idea of 'growing beyond'. *Is increasing* (*pleonazei*) is another strong verb; it differs in that, whereas the previous verb applies strictly to organic growth (like that of a healthy plant), this one points to wide dispersal. The *love* is exercised by the entire community and by each individual (*the love every one of you has for each other*). Paul has some salutary rebukes to administer, but he is glad to begin by paying his tribute to the Christian love that permeated the community.

In the first Epistle he had given thanks for their 'endurance inspired by hope' (1 Thes. 1:3), as well as for their faith and love. But the omission here is not significant, for he uses the same word in the next verse (translated 'perseverance') as one of the things about which he boasts.

4. The result (*hōste, therefore,* indicates consequence) of the increase of faith and love was that Paul and his companions boasted of the Thessalonians to other Christians. Those who maintain that the tone of this letter is colder than that of the first have a problem with the emphatic expressions used here. Instead of the simple *we,* Paul has the emphatic 'we ourselves' (*autous hēmas*), while the verb translated *boast* (*enkauchasthai,* a compound here only in the New Testament) is not the simple verb Paul generally uses. The meaning appears to be that it was not the habit of the preachers to boast of their converts (in 1 Thes. 1:9 other people boast to Paul, not he to them); but in this case the merits are so outstanding that even the founders of the church are constrained to sing its praises.

They boast about the converts' *perseverance* (see comment on 1 Thes. 1:3, where it is translated 'endurance') and *faith*. *Faith* is here understood by some as 'faithfulness', 'fidelity', because of its connection with 'endurance', but the reason scarcely seems adequate. *Pistis* can denote 'fidelity', but in the New Testament it nearly always means 'faith' (see comment on 3:2). In the previous verse it has been used in this normal sense and there seems no reason for a different meaning here. Amid their difficulties they had preserved their trust in God (*cf.* comment on 1 Thes. 3:5).

Persecutions are assaults made on Christians specifically on account of their Christian profession; *trials* (*thlipsesin*) are more general, any of the tribulations and troubles they might meet, whether persecution or any other. The present tense, *you are enduring*, shows that the troubles were not past history but present at the time of writing.

5. There is a difficulty in that the 'persecutions and trials' seem on the face of it to deny rather than to prove *that God's judgment is right*. But we should not understand the *evidence* to be the sufferings (as Rutherford, 'these sufferings attest the equity of God'). It is not the persecutions but the attitude of the Thessalonians in their troubles that is the decisive thing. Such constancy and faith could come only from the action of God within them, and if God has so inspired them this is clear evidence that he does not intend them to come short of the final attainment of *the kingdom* (*cf.* Phil. 1:28, and comment on 1 Thes. 2:12). Perhaps we should also notice Simeon's view that we cannot think of iniquity as triumphing over a moral God: 'The very existence of such enormities' as persecution is then ' "a manifest proof," or demonstration that there will be "a righteous judgment of God".'[1]

Lightfoot understands the *judgment* (more exactly 'the righteous judgment', *tēs dikaias kriseōs*, only here in Paul, though Rom. 2:5 is similar and Bailey remarks 'the idea is basic in his thinking') in terms of 'the law of compensation by which

---

[1] Simeon, p. 377.

the sufferers of this world shall rest hereafter and the persecutors of this world shall suffer hereafter'. While this thought is certainly in mind (v. 6), the idea here is bigger. It is part of God's righteous judgment to use tribulations to bring his own people to perfection. The Greek construction (*eis to* with the infinitive) expresses purpose; the judgment is in order that they may be counted worthy of the kingdom. The verb *kataxioō* means not 'to make worthy' but 'to declare worthy', 'to count worthy' (like that other great Pauline word *dikaioō*, 'to justify' in the sense 'to declare as just'). The apostle is excluding human merit even in a passage where he is drawing attention to a noteworthy piece of endurance; he is emphasizing that attainment to the kingdom is not the result of human endeavour, but is due to the grace of God.

For which you are suffering does not mean 'in order to gain which' but 'on behalf of which', 'in the interest of which'. It is precisely the disinterested nature of their sufferings that afforded the evidence that God was in them.

B. DIVINE JUDGMENT (1:6–10)

Paul lays down the general principle on which judgment is based and proceeds to some truths about final judgment. Some have felt that there is too much of 'an eye for an eye' about this and they ascribe the words to a Jewish interpolator. Such a position cannot be sustained. There is no evidence and in any case the idea is fully Christian. In a moral universe sin cannot go unpunished. The sinner always hopes that he will escape penalty, but, because God is over all, this is quite impossible. 'Punishment is the other half of sin' (Denney).

6. Paul uses an 'if indeed' (*eiper*) construction, but this does not cast doubt on the proposition. It is a rhetorical understatement and is used of things as far beyond doubt as the indwelling of the Holy Spirit in the believer (Rom. 8:9) and the existence of idols (1 Cor. 8:5). NIV has simply *God is just,* and this is the force of it. Paul grounds the certainty of final judgment in the righteous nature of God. Because God is just we must expect the ultimate righting of wrongs; that God will repay 'seems an essential constituent of any teaching about God's judgement' (Best). Jesus taught that there would be 'woe' for some as well as blessing for others (Lk. 6:20–26). The verb *pay back* (*antapo-didōmi*) contains the notion of what is due (see comment on 1 Thes. 3:9, and for *trouble* see on 1 Thes. 1:6 where the same word is translated 'suffering').

7. The positive side of the retribution now succeeds the neg-ative, as Paul thinks of *relief* (*anesin*, which means release of tension; it was used of the slackening of a taut bowstring) for the *troubled*. He points his friends to the prospect of relief from the afflictions that tormented them. Some object that this is an unworthy motive, but such objections usually emanate from the comfortable. It is a matter of history that those who are passing through suffering for the Lord's sake do not, as a rule, despise the prospect of final blessedness. This is not the whole of the gospel, but it is an authentic part of it and we are not wise to overlook it. *To us as well* reminds us that Paul and his companions were likewise persecuted. It is 'a sigh on his own account' (Findlay, *CGT*).

From this point to the end of verse 10 the structure is so markedly rhythmical that some scholars feel that Paul is quoting from some Jewish Psalm. Way calls it the 'Hymn of the Second Coming'. Paul may be quoting, but the language is his and there is no real reason for denying the passage to him.

The first point is the coming of the Lord Jesus. Paul says literally 'in the revelation of the Lord Jesus'; it is not only that the retribution will take place when Christ is revealed: the ret-ribution is itself part of the revelation ('Revelation includes the vindication of righteousness', Ward). The final consummation is a *parousia* (1 Thes. 3:13, *etc.*); now we find that it is also *apokalypsis* (as in 1 Cor. 1:7; 1 Pet. 1:7, 13, *etc.*), *i.e.* an uncover-ing, a disclosure. It is the revelation of a Person at present concealed. He will come *in blazing fire*, a concept not frequent in the New Testament. But fire is often associated with the divine presence in the Old Testament (*e.g.* Ex. 3:2; Is. 66.15–16) and in Revelation (Rev. 1:13–14, *etc.*). Here it is the robe of the returning Lord. *His powerful angels* is better 'the angels of his power' (JB); the emphasis is not on the power of the angels but on that of the Lord. Indeed, Moore holds that, in the light of Mark 14:62, *power* 'could be Paul's way of referring to Jesus' divinity . . . Jesus is to be revealed with angels appropriate to and underlining his divine nature'.

8. *He will punish* points to an activity that belongs to God alone (Dt. 32:35), and its ascription to Christ shows that Paul regarded him as divine in the fullest sense (in vv. 5–6 he spoke of God as judge). The word means not arbitrary punishment, but something like 'he will do justice upon' (NEB).

There are separate articles with *those who do not know God* and (those who) *do not obey the gospel*. The most natural understanding of this is that there are two groups of people. Some are so sure of this that they see the Gentiles in the former expression and the Jews in the latter (*cf.* Way, 'on those heathen who ignore God, on those Jews who refuse obedience'). This, however, seems to be reading too much into the passage. Rather, *those who do not know God* means anyone, heathen or not, who is guilty of culpable neglect of such knowledge of God as God has made possible; it is the rejection of proffered light (as in 1 Thes. 4:5). Those who *do not obey the gospel* form a specific example of the foregoing; they reject the ultimate revelation of God's saving activity. It is to be borne in mind, too, that this whole passage is markedly Hebraic; in the manner of many Old Testament passages the second expression may simply take up and fill out the thought of the first (*cf.* Je. 10:25).

9. *They* translates the relative of quality (*hoitines*), meaning 'who are of such a kind as to'; they are fit for the penalty they will receive. *Will be punished* is more exactly 'will pay penalty', the last word (*dikē*) being from the same root as 'righteous' (*dikaios*); it is not a mindless infliction of vindictive punishment, but the meting out of merited desert. The penalty is given in some detail. *Destruction* means not 'annihilation' but complete ruin. It is the loss of all that makes life worth living. Coupled with *everlasting* (better 'eternal', as RSV), it is the opposite of eternal life. The exact expression occurs again in 4 Maccabees 10:15 (and nowhere else in the Greek Bible), where it is the lot of the wicked tyrant and is set over against the 'blessed death' of the martyr. It is being *shut out from the presence of the Lord*. The final horror of sin is that it separates the sinner from God (*cf.* Is. 59:2). *The majesty of his power* points to another aspect of the same thing, for *majesty* (better 'glory', *doxa*) means something like 'the visible manifestation of the greatness of God'. Notice the almost incidental, but very telling, reference to his strength. The Thessalonians were feeling the power of human oppressors, but Paul reminds them that there is One mightier (*cf.* Is. 2:10, 19, 21).

These solemn words make clear the utter finality of the lot of the wicked. As Denney says, 'If there is any truth in Scripture at all, this is true – that those who stubbornly refuse to submit to the gospel, and to love and obey Jesus Christ, incur at the Last Advent an infinite and irreparable loss. They pass into a night on which no morning dawns.'

10. The 'when' that introduces this verse (see RSV) is the indefinite *hotan*; the coming is certain, but its time is not known. Whenever it takes place its distinguishing characteristic will be glory; a glory, Paul says, that will be *in his holy people*. The expression is not an easy one (see Bailey for a convenient summary of the possibilities). The verb is a compound found in the New Testament again only in verse 12; its meaning is 'be glorified-in', and it is followed by another 'in'. The Lord will be glorious and his glory will be in his saints too (*cf.* 1 Jn. 3:2, 'when he appears, we shall be like him'). Masson, Thomas and others see the meaning that he will be glorified in the midst of his saints (*cf.* Ps. 89:7), but this seems less likely. The glory of the day will surpass anything we know (*to be marvelled at*); we will be lost in amazement.

The aorist participle, *those who have believed*, has caused some strange interpretations (Lightfoot notes one, 'the past tense is used here to denote that faith would then have been absorbed in sight and ceased to be'). It is better to see the aorist as pointing to the initial step of faith; believing then is synonymous with becoming a Christian. Paul is talking about Christ's people, those who have believed in him.

The construction at the end of the verse is awkward, something like 'to be marvelled at in all those who have believed because our testimony to (or on) you was believed in that day'. Hort found this so difficult that he took the extreme step of making a conjectural emendation (a thing he rarely did). He read *epistōthē*, 'was confirmed', for *episteuthē*, 'was believed', and this was accepted by Moffatt, *EGT*. It is better to accept Lightfoot's suggestion that the passage is elliptical and read 'in all them that believed, and *therefore in you*, because our testimony was believed in you' (better, '. . . our testimony to you was believed'). The preachers' testimony to the Thessalonians produced the desired result.

C. PAUL'S PRAYER (1:11–12)

This is not an actual prayer interjected into the argument as is quite common in Paul, but the apostle's assurance that he prays for his friends constantly and in these terms.

11. *With this in mind* probably refers to the whole of the preceding section. Paul's prayer for the Thessalonians grows out of his thanksgiving for them and his contemplation of the wonderful things to come. The prayer is that they may grow in things spiritual, and this is expressed in various ways. First, *count you worthy*. This is not a prayer that the converts will not fall away. Paul's attention is fixed on the glory at the end time and he prays that they will then be adjudged worthy of having been called, *i.e.* that during the intervening period they will live in such a way as to ensure this commendation. Best holds that *axioō* here means 'make worthy' rather than 'count worthy', but we should take the word in its normal sense (*cf.* v. 5). *Calling (klēsis)* usually means the initial act whereby God calls people to be his own (*e.g.* Eph. 4:1; Phil. 3:14), and this is probably meant here. But it is also likely that Paul has in mind the final consummation of that call. He speaks of *our God*, uniting his converts with himself in contemplating their common Master.

By his power will apply to both the following: Paul prays that the power of God will be seen in the good purpose and also in the work of faith. Neither is to be done in merely human strength. There is no *of yours* in the Greek and some have thought that it is God's purpose (*cf.* AV 'his'). But NIV is surely right. The expression is more literally 'good pleasure of goodness' (*eudokia agathōsynēs*) and the word for 'goodness' is never used of God elsewhere in the New Testament. It refers to human goodness and is part of the fruit of the Spirit (Gal. 5:22). Paul prays that God will bring about the goodness of will (*eudokia*) that leads to goodness of action. It is like the Anglican collect for Easter Day, 'We humbly beseech thee, that as by thy special grace preventing (*i.e.* preceding) us thou dost put into our minds good desires, so by thy continual help we may bring the same to good effect', as several commentators point out. Coupled with this is *every act prompted by your faith*. Except that it lacks the definite article, the expression is identical with that translated 'your work produced by faith' (1 Thes. 1:3, where see comment). Faith is not passive; it is ceaselessly active, appropriating God's blessings and using God's power for God's service.

12. The *name* in biblical times stood for the whole person; to 'glorify the name' was thus to exalt the person. Paul thus looks for the Thessalonians so to produce the qualities of Christian character that the Saviour who has produced such works of mighty power within them will be exalted. Some see in the glorification of the name of Christ a reference to the parousia (so Best), but, while the parousia is not out of mind, the primary emphasis at this point is on the quality of life produced in the Thessalonians by the indwelling Christ (Rigaux argues for the present). For being *glorified in you, and you in him, cf.* Jesus' own words (Jn. 17:1, 10, 21–23); they are to be glorified not 'with' him, but 'in' him, and he is to be in them. This is the closest of unions.

All this is *according to the grace of God*. Everything is ascribed to its basic cause in God. The Thessalonians do not have the power to bring glory to the Lord, but they can do this by *grace* (see comment on 1 Thes. 1:1). *Grace* emphasizes the favour God shows to the unworthy, a favour made available through the work of Christ, and further, the gifts he bestows on people.

The purpose of such gifts is that people may live the life just spoken of.

It is grammatically possible to understand *our God* as synonymous with *the Lord Jesus Christ*, since one article covers both; indeed, Nigel Turner says bluntly, ' "Our Lord and God Jesus Christ" would be the correct rendering'[1] (*cf.* GNB mg., 'our God and Lord Jesus Christ'). But *kyrios* (*Lord*) often occurs without the article, like a proper name. Most commentators take this sense here and understand the expression to refer to both the Father and the Son. This is probable, but the other possibility cannot be excluded. And in any case we should notice the closeness of Christ and God.

III. THE PAROUSIA (2:1-12)

As in the first Epistle, the main part of the letter begins in the second chapter, after the introductory prayer. Some of the converts had evidently taken up with enthusiasm erroneous ideas about the second coming. Paul writes to supplement what he had already told them by word of mouth (v. 5). It is unfortunate for us that we do not know what he had said to them, for what he writes contains many allusions to his oral teaching. This passage is probably the most obscure and difficult in the whole of the Pauline writings and the many gaps in our knowledge have given rise to extravagant speculations. We do not possess the key to everything said here, and it is well accordingly to maintain some reserve in our interpretations.[2]

A. THE DAY OF THE LORD NOT YET PRESENT (2:1-2)

1. Paul begins with the language of entreaty (*cf.* 1 Thes. 4:1; 5:12). His *hyper* combines the ideas of *concerning* (NIV) and 'on behalf of'; it is something like 'in the interests of the truth concerning . . .'. The solemnity is heightened by the use of the

---

[1] N. Turner, *Grammatical Insights into the New Testament* (T. & T. Clark, 1965), p. 16.
[2] On this whole section the admirable treatment in Geerhardus Vos, *The Pauline Eschatology* (Eerdmans, 1953), should be consulted.

full, formal title, *our Lord Jesus Christ*. *Coming* (*parousia*, see comment on 1 Thes. 2:19) and *being gathered* (*episynagōgē*; elsewhere in the New Testament only in Heb. 10:25, of the gathering of Christians for worship) are combined under one article; the two are closely connected and are parts of one great whole (*cf.* 1 Thes. 4:16–17).

2. Paul looks for his friends to be settled in mind (*cf.* Eph. 4:14). His verb *saleuthēnai* (*become . . . unsettled*) may be used of the motion produced by wind and wave; it indicates a restless tossing, as of a ship not securely moored or even shaken loose from its moorings. Paul does not want the converts to be shaken 'from the mind' (omitted in NIV; this passage is cited in BDF 211 as one where *apo* is 'used to designate separation, alienation'). The mind (*nous*) stands for the mental aspect of man, but the mind considered as the reason, the whole mental balance, rather than as the mechanism of thought. The aorist infinitive points to a sudden shock that throws them off balance. *Or alarmed* (*throeisthai*) is a change to the present infinitive and denotes a continuing state of agitation (*cf.* Mk. 13:7); it points to an ongoing anxiety. Paul warns against both a sudden jolt and a continuing state of remaining upset.

He lists three things that might bring this about. *Prophecy* (or 'spirit', *pneuma*) means a supernatural revelation, and *report* (or 'word', *logos*) an oral communication of some sort, perhaps a sermon. The *letter* may refer to 1 Thessalonians (which in that case has been misunderstood), to some other letter Paul had written, or to a forgery put out in his name. Some commentators take *supposed to have come from us* to apply only to *letter* (*e.g.* EGT), but it is more likely that it applies to all three. The meaning will then be, 'Perhaps it is thought that we said this while prophesying or preaching, or that we wrote it in a letter' (GNB). The expression *supposed to have come from us* (*hōs di' hēmōn*) is rather vague; perhaps Paul was not quite sure what had happened or did not care to define it too closely. What is beyond dispute is that he vehemently denies that he has done anything to give currency to the report in question.

That report is *that the day of the Lord has already come*. The verb is *enestēken*, which is often used of present activities such as 'the current month', 'the present day' (see MM); Paul employs it in distinguishing the present from the future (Rom. 8:38; 1 Cor. 3:22). Obviously the Lord had not returned visibly (as outlined in 1 Thes. 4:16–17). But *the day of the Lord* was a complex that included many events. The report would mean that this series of events had already begun to unfold (perhaps the sufferings of the Thessalonians were said to show this). If so, the 'Day' was already present; the exciting culmination was very close.[1] Jesus had warned against a somewhat similar expectation (Mk. 13:7).

B. THE GREAT REBELLION (2:3–12)

1. The man of lawlessness (2:3–10a)
Paul speaks of the great opposition to God and God's people that will precede the day of the Lord.

3. The Thessalonians must not be deceived *in any way*, whether by the things listed in verse 2 or by anything else whatever. The construction is broken in the following clause, but NIV is surely right in supplying the words *that day will not come*. While the coming of 'the day of the Lord' will be unexpected (1 Thes. 5:2–3), certain things will precede it. One is *the rebellion*. The definite article shows that the rebellion was well known to the readers; evidently it had formed part of Paul's previous teaching. Our difficulty is that we do not know what he had told them. In classical Greek *apostasia* meant a political or military rebellion, but in LXX it is used of rebellion against God (*e.g.* Jos. 22:22), and this became the accepted biblical usage. Paul is saying that in the last times there will be a great uprising of the powers of evil against God (*cf.* Mt. 24:10ff.; 1 Tim. 4:1–3; 2 Tim. 3:1–9; 4:3–4). It is as though Satan were throwing all his forces into one last despairing effort.

---

[1] Some recent studies suggest that a form of Gnosticism is in mind (*e.g.* Schmithals). W. Marxsen holds that 'a Gnostic idea is being expressed apocalyptically' and reminds us of heretics who spoke of the resurrection as past (2 Tim. 2:18) (*Introduction to the New Testament* (Fortress, 1974), p. 39). But there is no real evidence that Gnosticism was as early as this. Further, this is not a natural understanding of what Paul says.

A feature of the rebellion will be the appearance of *the man of lawlessness*. Some MSS read 'man of sin' (GNB 'the Wicked One'); *lawlessness* seems to be the correct reading, but there is no great difference in meaning, for 'sin is lawlessness' (1 Jn. 3:4). In the Bible the essence of sin is not its ethical quality, but the fact that it is rebellion against God; it is the assertion of the will of man against that of God. *The man of lawlessness* will be *revealed*, which points to his existence before his manifestation (*cf.* the revelation of Christ, 1:7). But this does not necessarily mean, as some commentators hold, that he must have been in existence at the time Paul was writing, only that his beginning does not coincide with his manifestation. An evil power is at work (v. 7), but this is not necessarily *the man of lawlessness*.

It is difficult to say who this *man of lawlessness* is, and there have been many suggestions, usually some outstandingly evil person at the time of the suggestion. Throughout history there have been many who have done Satan's evil work (*cf.* the 'many antichrists', 1 Jn. 2:18), and this is a warning against over-hasty identification of the man of this chapter with any historical personage. Paul's concern is not with the evil ones who appear from time to time, but with the most infamous of all, one who will appear in the last days. He never uses the term 'Antichrist', but plainly he has in mind the being John calls by this name. He is not Satan, for he is distinguished from him (v. 9); but he is Satan's instrument, imbued with Satan's spirit.

He is also called *the man doomed to destruction* ('the Lost One', JB), an expression used also of Judas Iscariot (Jn. 17:12), of whom it is said that he 'left to go where he belongs' (Acts 1:25).

4. The language here is like that in a number of passages in Daniel (see Dn. 7:25; 8:9–12; 11:36–37), but Paul is not simply reproducing the thought of Daniel. His mind was steeped in the language of the Old Testament and he naturally made use of it on such an occasion as this. But he is describing a different figure, the leader of the forces of evil in the last time. *He opposes* renders a participle which might well be translated 'the opposer' or 'the adversary', a term sometimes applied to Satan (*e.g.* 1 Tim. 5:14; NIV 'the enemy'); indeed, the Hebrew word *satan* means 'adversary' (*cf.* Zc. 3:1). The use of the term emphasizes the kinship of the 'man of lawlessness' with his master. Closely joined with this is a second participle (there is but one article in the Greek), 'the exalter of himself'. The verb (*hyperairomai*) is found elsewhere in the New Testament only in 2 Corinthians 12:7 (where AV twice translates it 'exalted above measure'). *Everything that is called God* seems wide enough, for it includes the true God and any so-called god, but it is further extended by *or is worshipped* (*sebasma* includes all kinds of objects of veneration, such as shrines, images, altars, *etc.*).

The 'man of lawlessness' *even sets himself up in God's temple*, claiming divine honours. Some understand this to mean the setting up of an image within the shrine, like the Emperor Caligula's attempt to set up an image of himself in the temple at Jerusalem (only his death stopped the project). But the language rather indicates that the man will sit in the holy place in person; *cf.* Jesus' words about 'the abomination that causes desolation' (Mk. 13:14; the masculine participle shows that a person is meant). An important feature of the rebellion in the last days will be the attempt to dethrone God. The evil person will proclaim that he is God (*cf.* Ezk. 28:2; Acts 12:21–23). Some think that *God's temple* means 'the church' (*cf.* 1 Cor. 3:16), but it is more likely that something like the temple in Jerusalem is meant.

5. None of this was new to the Thessalonians, for it had formed part of the original preaching; the imperfect tense (*elegon*) may mean *I used to tell you*, or, as Rutherford puts it, 'I often spoke of this'. Paul had evidently spoken much about the second coming in his original preaching, and he expected the Thessalonians to recognize his allusions accordingly. He uses the first person singular, instinctively recalling his personal contribution to the preaching.

6. *And now* may be logical (BDF 442 (15)), simply marking a transition (as in Acts 3:17, *etc.*); or it may be strictly temporal, 'and as concerns the present', forming a contrast with *at the proper time*. Probably the second alternative is to be preferred. There is the further question of whether we should take *now* with *know* or with *holding him back*. The Greek could mean either, but it seems better to take it with *know* (Bruce calls RSV's 'you know what is restraining him now' a solecism). Because they knew, Paul could content himself with an allusion, and because he did, we can only guess at his meaning. The words *what is holding . . . back* render the neuter participle of the verb *katechō* (the masculine participle occurs in the next verse, 'the one who . . . holds . . . back'). The verb can mean (a) 'to hold fast' (as in 1 Thes. 5:21), (b) 'to hold back' (as in Phm. 13), (c) 'to hold sway' (if intransitive).

D. W. B. Robinson argues for this third meaning,[1] but the verb does not have this meaning elsewhere in the New Testament and not many have been convinced. Most commentators accept the sense 'to hold back'; Paul is saying that the appearance of 'the man of lawlessness' is impossible at the present, for there is a restraining power (and in v. 7 a restraining person).

An easy identification of the restrainer is the Roman Empire, which might be referred to in terms of itself, or in terms of the Emperor who personified it (the masculine may be used of a class as well as of an individual, *e.g.* Eph. 4:28). But the Roman Empire has long since passed away and the lawless one has not appeared. These days many think of an allusion to some angelic being familiar in contemporary eschatological speculations; if so, we have no way of knowing, for we no longer have those eschatological speculations. An interesting suggestion is that the neuter refers to the preaching of the gospel (the end cannot come until the gospel is preached to all), and the masculine to Paul, who preached it. B. B. Warfield thought of the Jewish state,[2] though it is hard to reconcile this with Paul's attitude to the Jews (1 Thes. 2:14–16). Some have suggested the Father, or the Holy Spirit, but it is difficult to see in what sense either could be 'taken out of the way' (v. 7). Another suggestion is Satan, but this is surely excluded by verse 7, where the removal of the restraining power is the signal for the appearance of 'the man of lawlessness'. Dibelius thought it was something somewhere – Paul was not quite sure what – and he thus shifted

---

[1] *Studia Evangelica*, vol. ii, ed. F. L. Cross (Akademie-Verlag, 1964), pp. 635–638.
[2] B. B. Warfield, *Biblical and Theological Studies* (Presbyterian and Reformed, 1952), p. 473.

from the neuter to the masculine.[1]

But the plain fact is that we do not know. It is best honestly to admit this and not to try to force the passage into conformity with some theory we have evolved on the basis of imperfect knowledge. If we must make a choice, the best suggestion seems to be that it is the rule of law restraining the operation of evil in a well-ordered state. This can be thought of in itself or as personified in the ruler. It was illustrated in the Roman Empire and continues in other states; indeed, Roman law is to a large extent perpetuated in the legal systems of the states that succeeded the Empire. The Jewish law is another illustration of the principle, restraining the operation of sin (Gal. 3:19, 24). Perhaps we should bear in mind that John refers to 'the spirit of the antichrist' as well as 'the antichrist' (thus using both neuter and masculine); indeed, he refers to 'many antichrists' in whom that spirit finds expression (1 Jn. 4:3; 2:18). But he does not appear to be saying what Paul is saying, and, as we noted above, we really do not have the clue to Paul's complete meaning.

The reference to his being *revealed at the proper time* shows that God is in complete charge. When God's time has come, and not till then, 'the man of lawlessness' will make his appearance. Paul clearly thinks of the time as being in the hand of God.

7. The characteristic work of 'the man of lawlessness' is to oppose the things of God, and Paul sees this evil as already at work in the world (*cf.* 1 Jn. 2:18). But it cannot reach its consummation until the restraining power is removed. *Secret power* translates *mystērion* ('mystery', RSV). It does not mean a mystery in the sense of something hard to work out, but a secret we can never work out. In the New Testament the secret is usually one that has now been revealed (Mk. 4:11; Rom. 16:25; Col. 1:26). There are interesting phrases such as 'the mystery of the faith' (1 Tim. 3:9, RSV), and 'the mystery of godliness' (1 Tim. 3:16).

---

[1] Charles H. Giblin has a monograph on the problems of this chapter, *The Threat to Faith* (Pontifical Biblical Institute, 1957). This is a detailed discussion and Giblin has assembled a large amount of material. But his solutions do not attract. Thus he translates here 'the seizing power' and understands the expression of an evil force. There is a good discussion of the problems in Best, pp. 295–302.

Here the word is in an emphatic position, with the meaning, 'Revealed, I say, rather than called into existence; for in fact the evil is already working, though in secret' (Lightfoot).

8. *And then (tote)* indicates that these further events will follow more or less immediately after the removal of the restraining power. *The lawless one* is, of course, identical with 'the man of lawlessness', and now for the third time he is said to be *revealed*, which puts a certain emphasis on the supernatural aspect of his appearing.

Paul's primary aim is not to gratify curiosity about this being and he gives no details of his activity; he goes straight from his appearance to his destruction. Throughout this whole section there is the underlying note of God's unchallenged sovereignty; thus the revelation of *the lawless one* is naturally followed by his destruction (described in words reminiscent of Is. 11:4). The better MSS read 'slay' (*anelei*, cf. RSV) for 'consume' (*analōsei*, cf. AV), but the difference is not great. *The breath of his mouth* (here only in the New Testament; cf. Ps. 33:6) shows that, terrible though *the lawless one* will be, he cannot stand before the Lord for a moment. There will not even be a contest – the breath (or 'the word', Calvin) of God is sufficient (cf. Rev. 19:21).

There is a parallel thought: *and destroy by the splendour of his coming.* For the Lord even to show himself is to destroy the enemy. *Destroy* translates *katargēsei* (this verb is in Paul in 25 of its 27 occurrences), which has the basic meaning 'to make idle' and thus 'to render null and void'. It does not mean that *the lawless one* will be annihilated, but that he will be made completely powerless. *Splendour* translates *epiphaneia*, which means much the same as *coming (parousia)*. Indeed, in all the other five places where it occurs in the New Testament it refers to our Lord's coming, once to his first advent (2 Tim. 1:10), and four times to his second advent (1 Tim. 6:14; 2 Tim. 4:1, 8; Tit. 2:13). It often appears to include the idea of splendour, which is the reason for NIV's rendering (cf. Rutherford, 'the glory of his Presence'; Phillips, 'the radiance of the coming').

9. Just as the Lord has his coming, so *the lawless one* has his. Many commentators from the earliest times have pointed out that 'the man of lawlessness' at many points counterfeits the Christ. He will be working in the power of Satan as Christ was of God, and he will perform miracles of various kinds as did the Lord. The *work* (*energeia*) means more than power; it is power in action. *The lawless one* then will embody the power of Satan.

There is some difficulty about the second part of the verse. NIV takes *counterfeit* (*pseudous*, 'of a lie') with all three of the marvels; RSV 'all power and with pretended signs and wonders' takes it with the latter two; NASB 'with all power and signs and false wonders' links it with the last only. It seems that both *all* and *counterfeit* should be taken with all three. They all point to miracles, the first referring to the power at work in them, the second to their characteristic as being meaningful (they point to something beyond themselves), and the third to the effect they have on spectators as portents, things that cannot be explained. And all three, Paul says, are saturated with falsehood. RSV misinterprets with 'pretended'. For Paul the miracles are real enough; it is their origin and end that make the lie.

10a. The thought of the previous verse is continued. The 'lawless one' will work by the method of wicked deceit (literally, 'in all deceit of unrighteousness', *adikia*), an unrighteousness that is characteristic of him (*adikia* is unrighteousness in its widest aspect; it includes all forms of evil). But this deceit is effective only in *those who are perishing* (*cf.* 1 Cor. 1:18). The use of the present tense makes it vivid. Paul sees the process going on before his eyes.

2. The man of lawlessness's followers (2:10b–12)
Paul turns from 'the lawless one' to those so misguided as to follow him.

10b. These people *perish*. The reason is that *they refused to love the truth*, more exactly, 'they did not receive the love of the truth'. The verb implies welcome (see comment on 1 Thes. 2:13), but people like this give the gospel no welcome. 'The love of the truth' is unusual (found only here in the Greek Bible), and it is placed in an emphatic position. We should not under-

133

stand *truth* as an abstract moral quality, but as 'the truth of the gospel' (Gal. 2:14), 'the word of truth, the gospel' (Col. 1:5), truth that is closely connected with Jesus (Jn. 14:6; Eph. 4:21), and which is revealed by God and comes from God (*cf.* Rom. 1:25). Acceptance of this truth leads to salvation (as the end of the verse shows). These people received some knowledge of God's way, but they would have none of it. They gave it no welcome; they gave it no love. And this in spite of the fact that the truth was the only way whereby they might have been saved. Calvin points out that those who perished 'were deserving of it, nay more, did of their own accord *choose death'*.

11. The ascription of the delusion to God, not Satan, is startling to modern Westerners. But in the Bible the sovereignty of God is clear and this takes unexpected forms. Thus God is said to have put a lying spirit into the mouths of the false prophets (1 Ki. 22:23; *cf.* Ezk. 14:9); again, one and the same action can be ascribed both to Satan (1 Ch. 21:1) and to God (2 Sa. 24:1). In Hebrew thought the powers of evil have no independent existence, but always depend on God. He makes the wrath of man to praise him (Ps. 76:10, see RSV), and he works his purposes out even in the evil that people (or Satan) do. In particular, God uses the evil consequences of sin in his punishment of the sinner. These consequences are not simply the result of the operation of an impersonal process; Paul can say that God gave people up to the consequences of their sin (Rom. 1:24, 26, 28; *cf.* 11:8). God's hand is in the process whereby the sinner receives the fitting recompense of sin. But we should not miss the point that even in dealing with disobedience God's purpose is mercy (Rom. 11:32).

Paul sees God's hand in the process whereby those who reject the gospel come to believe a lie. *For this reason* refers us back to the statement that certain sinners refused to receive the love of the truth. It is the law of life that those who take this step go further and further into error. Paul puts some emphasis on the word *God*; what follows is not the result of mere chance or the working of natural law, but of divine action. The present tense (*sends*) referring to future action is the prophetic present, giving a note of greater certainty. It is not easy to translate *energeian planēs* (*a powerful delusion*). As we saw on verse 9, *energeia* means power in action, so that the expression signifies not merely a passive acquiescence in wrong-doing, but an active forwarding of evil. When people begin by rejecting the good, they end by forwarding the evil.

The upshot of this is *that they will believe the lie*. This lie stands over against the truth of verse 10; it stands for what Satan would have people believe, more particularly with regard to 'the lawless one'. That is *the* lie (*cf*. Rom. 1:25). But those who reject the gospel of God are bound to end by accepting the evil as true. Thereby God uses Satan as his means of punishing them. This is not a contest between God and Satan in which God turns out to be a little stronger than Satan. God is sovereign over all, and uses even evil (in Satan and in people) to set forward his purpose.

12. This is further explained in a second clause of purpose: *so that* (*hina*) *all will be condemned* (NASB 'judged' reminds us that justice is involved). God brings them to their condemnation by their acceptance of the lie. They think this acceptance is the end of the story (sinners do not see beyond the sin they are enjoying). But it is not. In the purposes of God it necessarily leads to condemnation.

Those condemned *have not believed the truth*. Paul often uses the verb 'to believe', but the construction here (with the dative of person) is found in the Pauline writings elsewhere only twice apart from quotations (2 Tim. 1:12; Tit. 3:8). Paul prefers a construction that conveys the meaning, 'put one's trust in', whereas that used here simply means to give credence. Far from welcoming the gospel, these people did not even accept as true ('believe') the truth of God.

More than that: they *delighted in wickedness*. The picture is one of people who have rejected the light God has given them and turned their backs on the love of the truth. This cannot be done without consequences; they become immersed in their lower pursuits and come to the position where they take their delight in them. So far have they become perverted from their true end (defined for us in *The Shorter Catechism* as 'to glorify God, and to enjoy him for ever') that, instead of enjoying God, they enjoy sin. For them evil has become good.

IV. THANKSGIVING AND ENCOURAGEMENT (2:13-17)

A. THANKSGIVING (2:13-15)

13. Paul turns to the bright future which, by contrast with that of 'the lawless one' and his followers, awaits his Thessalonian friends. In words reminiscent of 1:3, he emphasizes the obligation that rests on him and his companions to give thanks continually for what God has done in and for the converts. The word order, with its stress on obligation, may be an intentional recalling of the language of the opening of the Epistle, and a re-emphasizing of the point that any modest disclaimer of the Thessalonians that they were unworthy of the praise accorded them in the first Epistle was out of place. The writers simply *had* to give thanks for the very real work of God so plainly manifest in these humble believers.

They are *brothers loved by the Lord* (*cf.* 1 Thes. 1:4), where *Lord* means Jesus. Paul uses this term often and it is specially appropriate here, where he has been speaking of the might of Antichrist. Those *loved by the Lord* have nothing to fear from such a one. Paul is not setting out a doctrine of the Trinity, but all three Persons are mentioned (as in Mt. 28:19; 1 Cor. 12:4–6; 2 Cor. 13:14; Eph. 4:4–6; Heb. 9:14; 1 Pet. 1:2; Jude 20–21).

Paul gives thanks for the election of the Thessalonians and uses an unusual word for *chose* (*heilato*); it is not found elsewhere in the New Testament in this sense (though it is used in LXX of the choosing of Israel in Dt. 26:18, and in a compound form in Dt. 7:6–7; 10:15). Several words are employed for election, which may indicate that it is many-sided. The Thessalonians were chosen *from the beginning*, which Findlay and others understand as the beginning of the preaching of the gospel in Thessalonica. This exact expression is not found elsewhere in Paul, but other writers use it for the beginning of all things (*e.g.* Mt. 19:4; 1 Jn. 2:13), and the idea that election took place before the world is familiar in Pauline writings (*cf.* Eph. 1:4). We should take it this way here (*cf.* NEB 'from the beginning of time'). Some

MSS read 'first-fruits' (*aparchēn* rather than *ap' archēs*), and this is accepted by Moffatt, Bruce, Whiteley, GNB, *etc.* But the evidence favours *from the beginning*.

Election is 'for salvation' and this is further defined as *through the sanctifying work of the Spirit and through belief in the truth*. The first expression points us to the setting apart of the whole person for the service of God, something that can be accomplished only in the power of the Holy Spirit (*cf.* 1 Thes. 1:5; 1 Pet. 1:2). The second is concerned rather with the response of faith to the gospel (understanding *truth* as in vv. 10, 12). The combination brings out the primary function of the Holy Spirit, but also the necessity for our response.

14. Paul moves from the eternal purpose in the mind of God ('from the beginning') to the manifestation of that purpose in time (*he called you*) and its future consummation (*in the glory; cf.* Rom. 8:28–30; 1 Thes. 2:12; 5:24). The divine call is of central importance. Paul uses the term 'call' with the implication that it has not only been made, but answered. The terminology of the Gospels is different; there many may be 'called' but few 'chosen' (*e.g.* Mt. 22:14). But, while the terminology is different, the essential idea is not, and the primacy of the divine is clear in both. For *our gospel* see comment on 1 Thessalonians 1:5.

Sharing *in the glory* is not something additional to salvation (v. 13), but a filling out of part of its content. For *share* see the note on *peripoiēsis* (1 Thes. 5:9). *The glory of our Lord Jesus Christ* is in view in all the gospel; when people receive the gospel they become sharers in Christ's glory (*cf.* Jn. 17:22; Rom. 8:17). That glory has already been manifested in part (Jn. 1:14; 13:31), but its fullness is yet to appear (see 1:10 and comment).

Denney speaks of these last two verses as 'a system of theology in miniature', a statement justified by the richness of their content. Important aspects of the Christian message are not mentioned, such as the cross and the resurrection, but they are implied in what is said. And for people subject to the difficulties and perplexities of the Thessalonians, what is said must have been extremely satisfying.

15. *So then (ara oun;* see comment on 1 Thes. 5:6), since God has so clearly included you in his great purpose, and since that purpose cannot be defeated even by Satan and 'the lawless one', *brothers* (note the affectionate address in this serious exhortation), *stand firm*, neither frightened by the magnitude of the opposition, nor unsettled by uncertainties about the details of the end. Paul is appealing to the known truth of the gospel as a safeguard against being stampeded by the kind of thing his friends found difficult.

Paradoseis, translated *teachings* but better 'traditions' (NASB, NEB, JB, *etc.*), draws attention to the derivative nature of the gospel (*cf.* 1 Cor. 11:23; 15:3). It stands for all Christian teaching, oral or written. The essential thing is that it is handed on by one to another and that it was received in the first place from God. 'The prominent idea of *paradosis* . . . is that of an authority external to the teacher himself' (Lightfoot). Milligan points out that the word is used in the inscriptions of 'Treasure Lists and Inventories . . . the articles enumerated being "handed over" '. This is another way of putting the truth (insisted on in 1 Thes. 2:13, *etc.*) that the gospel is not of human origin; the preacher is never at liberty to substitute his own thoughts for what he has received. The traditions came both *by word of mouth* and *by our* (*hēmōn*) *letter* (probably 1 Thessalonians). It does not matter in which form God's word was delivered. Either way it was authoritative.

B. PRAYER FOR THE CONVERTS (2:16–17)

16. As in the first Epistle, Paul brings the main section of the letter to a close with a prayer for the Thessalonians (*cf.* 1 Thes. 3:11–13), and some of the wording is markedly similar. He places *our Lord Jesus Christ himself* before *God our Father*, probably because the Lord Jesus has been much in mind in the preceding section. Paul's usual habit is to mention the Father first, but the order is sometimes reversed, as in the well-known 'grace' (2 Cor. 13:14; *cf.* Gal. 1:1). The facts that the Lord Jesus is so closely associated with the Father, and that on occasion he is placed first, are evidence of the way Paul thought of him. Clearly he did not distinguish him sharply from the Father and this is seen in the fact that the verbs 'encourage' and 'strengthen' in the next verse are both singular, despite the double subject. Paul saw the Father and the Son as in some sense one (see also on 1 Thes. 3:11).

After *God our Father* Paul has two participles linked with a common article (*loved* and *gave*); these probably refer to the Father only, although it is grammatically possible that they refer also to the Son. Both are in the aorist, which seems to mean that *loved* refers primarily to the manifestation of the love at Calvary, and that *gave* likewise points to God's initial gift. *Eternal encouragement* underlines the thought that this good gift of God is lasting; it cannot be shaken by anything now or through eternity. The eschatological note is continued in *good hope*. The religions of the day found little place for hope, but hope rings through the New Testament, and it is much more than the mild optimism that often passes for hope in modern times. In the New Testament hope has something of the note of certainty about it, because it is grounded in the divine nature and rests on the divine promises. Here it is the gift of *grace* (see comment on 1 Thes. 1:1), and a hope based on God's grace can never be disappointed (*cf.* Rom. 5:5). It is a *good* hope, not confined to minor issues of the here and now, but reaching over into the coming age.

17. For the singular verbs see comments on verse 16 and for their meanings those on 1 Thessalonians 3:2. Paul prays for a comprehensive strengthening of his converts; *every good deed and word* includes all things, great and small. The Christian is to be busy. As Barclay says, 'The Christian is not called to dream, but to fight. . . . He is called not only to the greatest privilege in the world, but also to the greatest task in the world.' *Hearts* refers to the depths of the inner being; Paul is praying that his friends will be strengthened inwardly, at the very core.

V. THE FAITHFULNESS OF GOD (3:1–5)

Paul is sure of God's faithfulness and in this certainty he looks for his friends to pray for him. He goes on to show his confidence that God will do great things.

A. REQUEST FOR PRAYER (3:1–2)

1. *Finally* (*to loipon*; see comment on 1 Thes. 4:1) brings us to the concluding part of the letter. It does not mean that there is nothing more to say, for Paul could and did discuss weighty matters after it. But it does mean that the main argument is concluded. Here it leads to a request for prayer (as in 1 Thes. 5:25). The verb *pray* is in an emphatic position (the subject is important), and it is in the present tense, which means 'Pray continually'. Some think that Paul had been told that the converts were praying for him and that he responds with emphasis, 'Keep on praying (as you are doing).' Or he may mean, 'Not only hold fast our teachings (2:15), but also pray for us.' But we should not read too much into a tense; Paul often asks people to pray for him and this may simply be a reflection of his deep sense of need; he depended on God and he thus needed constant prayer.

That the message of the Lord may spread rapidly is more exactly 'that the word of the Lord may run'. Paul sees 'the word' as active and vigorous, moving swiftly to accomplish God's purpose. The imagery goes back to Psalm 147:15 (*cf.* also Ps. 19:4–5), and the Greek games may also be in mind, for Paul often uses illustrations from these athletic contests. 'May run' refers to what the word does in itself, while *be honoured* (or 'glorified') is concerned rather with its effect on people. When people see what God's word accomplishes they will glorify it, as the Gentiles in Pisidian Antioch did (Acts 13:48). There is no *it was* in the Greek; Paul says 'just as also with you'. Translators usually help him out with *it was* (as NIV), making him refer to the time of the original mission, or 'it is' (AV), making the reference to the time of writing. More likely it includes both. Paul was having difficulties in Corinth, and he recalls with nostalgia the Thessalonian mission (*cf.* 1 Thes. 1:5–10; 2:1, 13) and Timothy's later report (1 Thes. 3:6–7). In Thessalonica the word of God was not bound (*cf.* 2 Tim. 2:9), and Paul longs to see its swift and powerful action in Corinth too.

2. For *delivered* see comment on 1 Thessalonians 1:10 (where this verb is translated 'rescues'). There is an article with *wicked and evil men*, which points to a definite group (not adversaries of the gospel in general), as does the aorist tense in the verb. There can be no doubt that these people were the Jews who gave the apostle such trouble in Corinth (Acts 18:12ff.; *cf.* Rom. 15:31). *Wicked* translates *atopōn*, 'that which is out of place', thus 'improper', 'wicked'. This is the only place in the New Testament where it is used of persons (it refers to things in Lk. 23:41; Acts 25:5; 28:6). *Evil* (*ponērōn*) means not simply a passive acquiescence in badness, but an active evil. So Paul looks to his friends to pray that he will be delivered from wicked people who would oppose the gospel and harm its ambassadors.

There is dispute about the meaning of *not everyone has faith*, for *pistis* may mean 'faith' in the sense of belief and trust, or 'faithfulness', 'fidelity', or, with the article (which it has here), 'the faith', the body of Christian teaching. When the word is used of God it always has the second meaning, but it is doubtful whether it ever has this sense in the New Testament when it is used of people. In this passage there is not a great deal of difference between 'not all people have faith (trust)' and 'not all people accept the Christian faith (teaching)'. Either way Paul is clearly stressing that his opponents came from among those to whom the great Christian verities mean nothing. But *faith* is more likely than 'the faith' in a letter as early as this, and it leads more naturally to what follows; we should understand the term as NIV.

B. GOD'S FAITHFULNESS (3:3–5)

3. The first word of this verse (*pistos*) is akin to the last word of the previous verse (*pistis*), and like it has more than one meaning. It may mean 'believing' in the sense of exercising faith, or 'faithful' in the sense 'reliable'. Clearly here it has the second sense. Paul is reminding his friends of the faithfulness of God (*cf.* 2 Tim. 2:13; for a similar play on words see Rom. 3:3).

We would have expected 'who will strengthen us', but Paul says 'who will strengthen you'. His deepest concern is for his flock, and he quickly passes over from his need to theirs. Notice the certainty with which Paul looks for strengthening (for this verb see comment on 1 Thes. 3:2), grounded as it is in the divine nature. *Protect* is really 'guard' (*phylassō*), and adds an important point. God will not establish his people and leave them; he will guard them continually. NIV is probably correct in translating *the evil one*, but the word is ambiguous and could mean 'evil' in general (there is a similar ambiguity in the Lord's prayer). Two things indicate that it is masculine here. First, this is by far the more common use in the New Testament; secondly, a reference to a person seems more likely in this context than to a principle. In the previous chapter Satan and his dupes have been in mind, and in the previous verse Paul was speaking of evil men. Everything points to a person here, and it seems that Paul is saying, 'God will guard you from all the assaults of Satan.'

4. Again we have an expression that can be understood in more ways than one. We may take *confidence* with *in the Lord* (as NIV, NASB, *etc.*), with *we* (JB 'we, in the Lord, have every confidence'), or with *you* (GNB 'the Lord gives us confidence in you'). In the end not much hangs on our decision, for Paul is resting his confidence in the Lord, and he is saying that this gives him confidence also in the Thessalonians. Because God is faithful and perfects that which he begins in those who trust him (see Phil. 1:6), Paul knows that he can rely on the Thessalonians. He is confident that they are obedient to what he commands (see comment on 1 Thes. 4:11), and that they will continue to be obedient. He does not say what these commands are and some connect them with the obligation to pray for the missionaries (v. 1). But much more probably he is leading up to the commands of verses 6ff. (notice the repetition of *command* in v. 6).

5. Paul's confidence in God leads him into a characteristic short prayer. *The Lord* is Jesus, as throughout this section. *Direct* (*kateuthynō*) means 'to make straight', and may be used of

·removing obstacles from the path (1 Thes. 3:11). The prayer is that Christ will open up the way for the whole of the inner life of the Thessalonians (for *hearts* see comments on 1 Thes. 2:4; 3:13) to be concentrated on the love and steadfastness of which he proceeds to speak.

There is dispute as to whether we should understand 'the love of God' as our love for God or as God's love for us (NIV), and similarly with 'the perseverance of Christ'. Paul's normal use would lead us to expect 'God's love for us' (he generally uses the verb when he refers to people loving God); on the other hand, in a prayer we would expect a petition that his readers should love God. But the construction is not precise; perhaps the primary thought is that of God's love for us, with the further thought that we should respond with an answering love. We should similarly think of *Christ's perseverance* as inspiring perseverance in his followers. It has been translated 'endurance' (1 Thes. 1:3, where see comment); it means 'the characteristic of a man who is unswerved from his deliberate purpose and his loyalty to faith and piety by even the greatest trials and sufferings' (GT). Paul is reminding his readers of the steadfast endurance Christ displayed and praying that they, in their measure, will reproduce the same.

VI. GODLY DISCIPLINE (3:6–15)

A. THE DISORDERLY (3:6–13)

The importance of this subject may be gauged from the fact that, next to that on the second coming, this is the longest section in the Epistle. If we compare the treatment of the subject in the first letter (1 Thes. 5:14) with what we have here, it is obvious that the problem has continued unabated or even intensified.

6. Paul's opening is authoritative; there is a military ring about the words he uses. Thus *command* is often used of a general giving orders to his troops, and 'disorderly' (NIV *idle*) refers to the failure of a soldier to keep in rank (see comment on 1 Thes.

5:14). The command is given *in the name of the Lord Jesus Christ* (*cf.* 1 Cor. 5:4), which makes it as authoritative as it possibly can be. But despite the authoritative tone, Paul uses the affectionate address *brothers* and applies it to the offenders as well as to other church members. They are to be dealt with, but they remain brothers. This is the warm affection of a friend, not the cold rule of an autocrat.

Paul enjoins the brothers *to keep away* from such people. His verb (*stellesthai*) was earlier used for activities such as furling sails. It signifies a withdrawing into oneself, a holding aloof (BAGD). But such a withdrawal is not to be made in a spirit of superiority. Paul appeals to brotherliness, and it is part of being a brother that no member should condone the deeds of another who, while claiming to be a brother, denies by his actions what the brotherhood stands for. Corporate responsibility is important.

When he was in Thessalonica Paul had warned against idleness; now he reminds his readers that such conduct is 'not according to the tradition' (NIV mg.; see comment on 2:15). *Live* is more exactly *walk* (*peripateō*), a metaphor Paul often uses for the steady progress that should characterize the Christian. There is a textual problem at the end of the verse, with some MSS reading *you received from us* (NIV, *etc.*) and others 'we gave them' (GNB). Either way Paul is saying that the church as a whole and the offenders in particular knew that this conduct was blameworthy, for they had received 'the tradition'. They knew that Paul had spoken on the subject in his original proclamation.

7. This is not new and Paul appeals to what *you yourselves* (*autoi; cf.* NASB, GNB) *know*. In the first letter he spoke of the example he and his companions had set (1 Thes. 1:5–6; 2:3ff.); now he goes further and says that the converts must follow that example. Paul's verb (*dei*) means more than *you ought* (NIV); it denotes a compelling necessity, 'you must'. *To follow our example* is better 'to imitate us' (JB; the verb is *mimeisthai*). The Thessalonians had been excellent imitators in some things (1 Thes. 1:6; 2:14); they must now extend the activity. The verb translated *we were not idle* (*ētaktēsamen;* the meaning is 'to be undisciplined', LSJ) is found here only in the New Testament, but there are other words from the same root in verses 6, 11 (and in 1 Thes. 5:14). In none of these passages is the meaning a general lack of discipline; it is the specific failure to earn one's living.

8. The expression 'to eat bread' (*arton*; NIV *food*) is a Hebraism; it comes to mean eating food generally (2 Ki. 4:8) and then to getting maintenance (2 Sa. 9:7). Paul is not saying that he did not get free meals, but that he refused to impose on anyone for his livelihood (*cf.* 1 Thes. 2:9). There is a difference from the statement in the first Epistle, for there he was professing the purity of his motives, while here he is appealing to the force of his example. Frame points out that, whereas Paul might have said that he had worked to set them an example, he increases the effect by pointing out two things: first, that his labour among them had been hard, constant and purely in their interests, and secondly that, while he had had the right to maintenance from the church, he had not exercised that right.

9. *Right* translates *exousia*, a word that originally meant freedom to do as one pleases, and came to mean authority or right. Milligan cites examples of its use in the papyri in wills and contracts in the sense of legal 'right'. Paul is insisting that, as a preacher, he had the full right to be maintained, an attitude he takes up in other places. His ideas on this subject are most fully developed in 1 Corinthians 9:3–14 (*cf.* 1 Tim. 5:17–18), where he bases the right to maintenance on a command of the Lord (*cf.* Mt. 10:10; Lk. 10:7). More than once Paul declined to exercise this right, but he never forgot that he had it.

At Thessalonica he waived his right in order to set the converts a good example. There was a whole-hearted commitment, for Paul says literally 'that we might give ourselves': notice two significant things, the verb 'give' and the emphatic *ourselves*. He might have said (as Rutherford actually translates), 'that you might have in us a pattern' (*cf.* GNB, 'we did it to be an example'). For *model* see comment on 1 Thessalonians 1:7.

10. *For even* is better 'For also': not only did we give you an

145

example when we were with you, but we also gave you a rule in concise form. *We gave you this rule* ('This we commanded you') uses the same authoritative verb as in verses 4, 6; here it is in the imperfect tense with the meaning 'This we used to command you'. It was apparently a constant theme of teaching, not simply an isolated saying. Findlay says it is 'a Jewish proverb, based upon Gen. iii. 19' (*cf.* the passages cited by Strack-Billerbeck). Adolf Deissmann saw it as 'a bit of good old workshop morality, a maxim applied no doubt hundreds of times by industrious workmen as they forbade a lazy apprentice to sit down to dinner' (*LAE*, p. 314). Some see in it a Greek saying; some find it among the Jews (*cf.* Pr. 10:4); others try to trace it to a saying of our Lord (*cf.* his own example, Mk. 6:3). But, while it is the kind of saying that might have arisen anywhere, in point of fact we cannot find it prior to this passage (earlier sayings are of the 'He who does not work, does not eat' variety). It may well be that Paul himself coined it. What is clear is that we owe to Paul the fact that it has been given a religous imperative and imported into the Christian scheme of things. He is, of course, referring to voluntary choice, the man who *will not* (*ou thelei*) work, not to unemployment as a result of unwelcome economic conditions.

11. *We hear* shows that Paul was not making general comments, but had specific instances in mind. The present tense may mean 'We keep hearing' or it may be more or less equivalent to the perfect 'we have heard'. The expression is used naturally of hearing by word of mouth, but it may also refer to what comes in a letter, so it gives no indication of the source of Paul's information. He says *some among you* rather than 'of you', and his word order is 'some who walk among you', not 'some among you walk'. This way of putting it may be meant to indicate that the relationship of the idlers to the church was not what it should be (Paul has used the same words 'among you' in v. 7 with reference to the preachers who, of course, did not belong to the local church). Moore thinks that the expression 'shows up the problem as an open scandal and the responsibility not only of the idlers but also of those amongst whom they live'.

The report was that some were *idle* (see comment on v. 6). Paul has a play on words which NIV brings out in words not unlike Moffatt's 'busybodies instead of busy' (the verb *periergazomai* is found only here in the New Testament, but the cognate adjective is in 1 Tim. 5:13 in a context which brings out the meaning). Most accept the idea that it was the supposed nearness of the second advent that convinced the idlers that it was useless to work for a living, and this is supported by the interest in eschatology, so clear from these letters. But it is possible that it arose from the Greek dislike of manual labour (Christians were made free in Christ; why should they work like slaves?), or that some of the 'spiritually minded' felt that mundane daily labour was beneath them and that other church members should keep them while they concentrated on promoting the 'spiritual' life. That they were *busybodies* shows that they would not let others alone; they may have been trying to convince them of the rightness of their position, or this may simply be the result of idleness. Paul castigates their conduct.

12. The apostle has a few words for the idlers themselves. He speaks tactfully as to brothers; he does not address them directly ('you idlers'), but uses an impersonal form, *such people*. To *command* he adds *urge* (*parakaleō*, translated 'encourage' in 1 Thes. 3:2, where see comment), which softens it a little. This is the one place where Paul has this combination. Further his exhortation is *in* (not 'by') *the Lord Jesus Christ*, at one and the same time reminding them of the brotherly relationship that links them to other church members and of the high standards that were the consequence.

There are three points in Paul's exhortation. *Settle down* is better 'with quietness they work' (AV), where 'quietness' refers to an inner tranquillity in contrast to their present excited state; 'they work' to the necessity for some real labour on their part in line with the apostle's own practice (v. 8); and *the bread they eat* to the earning of their living. There may be some emphasis on 'their own' (*heautōn*) with *bread*, for they had been in the habit of eating other people's.

13. *And as for you* (*hymeis de*) is a strong contrast; it turns the exhortation away from the loafers towards the church at large. Whatever the loafers choose to do, the duty of the *brothers* is plain. It is possible that the conduct of the idlers had so annoyed some of the other church members that they had grown irritable and had acted otherwise than love would direct. But we have no evidence, and the words are sufficiently general to be applicable, even without such a specific cause. It is important to notice that the church at large has a responsibility to its dissident members.

The verb *enkakeō* (*tire*) originally meant 'to behave badly in', and then came to mean 'to be weary', 'to flag'. *Doing what is right* is the participle of the compound verb *kalopoieō*, found only here in the New Testament, though the two parts occur together several times (*e.g.* Rom. 7:21; 2 Cor. 13:7; and especially Gal. 6:9, where the thought is much the same as here). It signifies ' "doing the fair, the noble thing" rather than "conferring benefits" ' (Milligan). Milligan also thinks that *kalos* 'carries with it the thought not only of what is right in itself . . . but of what is *perceived* to be right'. Believers are to direct their conduct to the highest ends, and that without flagging.

B. THE DISOBEDIENT (3:14–15)

Paul evidently thinks it likely that some of the more obstinate will not obey his directions, so he adds a few words to deal with that situation. At the same time he makes them broad enough to cover all that he has said, not just the matter of idleness.

14. The word *obey* (*hypakouei*) properly means the action of one who, in the position of doorkeeper, comes to listen (*cf.* its use in Acts 12:13, where NIV translates 'answer the door'). It carries the idea of hearing, then of acting on what is heard. *This letter* is correct, though perhaps we should notice that Paul says 'the letter' and some take this with the following in the sense, 'If any does not obey our word, designate him by letter', *i.e.* write to Paul about him. This has little to commend it; the word order is against it, as is the use of the definite article which, at the close of a letter, often means the letter just written (*e.g.* Rom. 16:22; 1 Thes. 5:27). In any case Paul is concerned that the community should take action, not that he should be the one to do it.

Take special note of him, writes Paul. His verb (*sēmeioō*) was originally neutral, but came sometimes to have the note of disapproval of the person or thing noted, as it does here. It was used by the grammarians in a sense equivalent to our 'N.B.' (see MM), so that it means more than a cursory notice. Paul does not say how the person is to be marked out, only that this be done. *Do not associate with him* employs a double compound (*synanamignysthai*) with 'the first preposition *syn* denoting "combination," the second *ana* "interchange" ' (Lightfoot). It means literally, 'Don't mix yourselves up with him.' This very expressive word conveys the idea of familiar intercourse, which is thus prohibited in the case of the erring brother. This is something the community should note, for the church as a whole is concerned with the behaviour of its individual members (*cf.* James W. Clarke, 'Christianity is finally dependent, for its influence on and growth in the world, upon the character of its disciples', *IB*). The verb is used in only one other passage in the New Testament (1 Cor. 5:9–11), where it is added that one is not to eat with the offender. The course urged here is not so stringent, for it is only the exercise of familiar intercourse that is cut off. Paul is insisting that the erring one be regarded as a brother and treated in such a way as to bring him back. The action is not excommunication (as Calvin held), but *in order that he may feel ashamed* (and so brought to a change of mind and conduct).

15. The attitude of tenderness is insisted on; the man is still to be treated *as a brother*. Most translations have something like *Yet* as the first word (taking *kai* as equivalent to *kaitoi*). But Paul says 'And'; he is not proceeding to a contrasting thought, but continuing and amplifying what he has said. The order of his words is interesting. 'And warn' is his sequence of thought, but he puts the words about not being an enemy before those about admonishing. He may have had some fear that the more zealous would be too eager for drastic action. He makes it clear that the offender is still to be regarded as one of themselves. He has erred, indeed, and his sin must be brought home to him. But this is to be done entirely in a spirit of love, with a tender concern for the welfare of the one being disciplined (*cf.* 2 Cor. 2:7). It is reclamation, not the purging of the flock, that is in mind. *Warn* is elsewhere translated 'admonish' (1 Thes. 5:12, where see comment); it conveys the thought of blame for wrongdoing, but also that of an act basically friendly (in the spirit of Pr. 27:6; *cf.* 1 Cor. 4:14). It is symbolical that the last word to the loafers, in the Greek as in our translation, is *brother*.

VII. CONCLUSION (3:16–18)

16. As in the first Epistle, Paul reminds his readers that what he has been telling them to do cannot be achieved in merely human strength (see 1 Thes. 5:23). The emphatic *autos de* with which the verse opens turns their thoughts away from their own efforts to *the Lord . . . himself*. Paul usually speaks of 'the God of peace' (see comment on 1 Thes. 5:23), but he generally means Christ when he says 'the Lord'. On the whole it is likely that he means Christ by *the Lord of peace* (*cf.* Eph. 2:14), though, as we have seen in other places, he does not sharply differentiate between God and Christ.

Peace (see comment on 1 Thes. 1:1) is a comprehensive term for the prosperity of the whole man; Paul seeks nothing less for his friends. Its supernatural origin is indicated by its association with *the Lord*. True peace in the deepest sense comes only as God's free gift; man can never work it up by his own effort. *At all times* (as RSV, NEB, *etc.*) is no improvement on 'always' (AV) as a translation of *dia pantos* (being rather the rendering of *pantote*). The idea is that of a peace that remains constant and unbroken no matter what the trials; 'continually' (Moffatt, NASB) is the sense of it. It is accompanied by *in every way* (*en panti tropō*), which does refer to changing circumstances (LB 'no matter what happens'). The peace for which Paul prays will be there continually and it will not vary, however much outward circumstances and conditions may alter.

The Lord be with all of you is not a different prayer altogether.

The peace the Christian enjoys has no existence in its own right; it is possible only because of the presence of the Lord. It is because we know that the Lord is with us and that he will never forsake those whose trust is in him (*cf*. Heb. 13:5) that our peace remains unbroken (Jn. 14:27). The peace of the Christian *is* the presence of the Lord.

There may well be significance in the *all*. Paul prays for every one of them, the dissident brothers as well as the loyal and obedient.

17. As he comes to the end of the letter, Paul takes the pen himself to add a personal greeting. His custom appears to have been to dictate a letter to an amanuensis who wrote it down (*cf*. Rom. 16:22); then at some point near the end Paul took the pen and added a few words in his own distinctive handwriting. The point at which he did this varied. In Galatians he wrote several verses (Gal. 6:11), and he may have himself written the whole of a short letter such as that to Philemon (Phm. 19). But usually it would seem to be very near the end, and he sometimes draws attention to the fact (1 Cor. 16:21; Col. 4:18). The fact that he says nothing about it in other letters does not mean that he did not do it, only that he did not emphasize it. Deissmann has a facsimile of a letter dated AD 50 from a certain Mystarion, in which the body of the letter is in one hand and the final greeting and date in another, clearly that of Mystarion himself (*LAE*, pp. 170ff.). There is nothing to draw attention to it; if we had only a copy we would not know. Paul is saying that this is his practice.

The *distinguishing mark* is the sign by which the letter can be recognized as genuine. The term is cognate with a verb used for signing a letter, and whether it is this that is in mind or not, the authentication is meant. Paul adds, *This is how I write* (this is his handwriting; which would be a help to them in situations such as that behind 2:2). *In all my letters* shows that Paul wrote other letters that have not been preserved.

It may be that there is special significance in thus calling attention to the genuineness of this letter. It does not mean that this is the first letter to the Thessalonians, as some suggest. It would be natural to write in this way in a second letter if some doubt had arisen as to how they could be sure that a letter really did come from Paul. From 2:2 it is plain that some *distinguishing mark* was needed.

18. The conclusion to this letter is identical with that to the first Epistle, except that Paul adds the word *all*. We have already noticed his tender concern for the disorderly. Right to the end this concern is operative, and he uses a farewell that includes them with the others.